A CUP OF C

10 OF THE TOP DUI ATTORNEYS IN THE UNITED STATES

VALUABLE INSIGHTS YOU SHOULD KNOW IF YOU ARE CHARGED WITH A DUI

Good Luck

Phil Wakefield

Hunter Biederman, Esq.
Randy Van Ittersum

Rutherford Publishing House
PO Box 969
Ramseur, NC 27316
www.RutherfordPublishingHouse.com

Cover photo: John Roman Images/Bigstock.com

ISBN-10: 0692388370
ISBN-13: 978-0692388372

TABLE OF CONTENTS

ACKNOWLEDGEMENTS

We all want to thank our husbands and wives, fathers and mothers, and everybody who has played a role in shaping our lives and our attitudes.

To all the clients we've had the honor of working with, who shaped our understanding of the difficulty of this time for you and your families. It has been our privilege to serve each and every one of you.

INTRODUCTION

Contributing Author:

Randy Van Ittersum

Host & Founder – Business Leader Spotlight Show

Anybody can be charged with driving while impaired. ANYBODY! Whether you regularly enjoy an evening cocktail before dinner, an attitude adjustment with the gang from the office during 'happy hour,' or are a teetotaler; if you ever sit behind the wheel and propel a two-ton mass of metal down a public highway at any speed, you are at risk for a DWI charge. A DUI charge is likely to have a significant impact on many areas of your life; your income, your freedom, and your ability to get a new job.

What surprises most people is that you need not be drunk to be charged with DWI.

As you will learn from the accounts within the pages of this book, people are stopped, arrested and charged with this very serious crime every day, and for most defendants, this is the first and only time they have been pulled over and asked if they have been drinking. You will also learn from the contents of the chapters, that not all "clues" police officers look for and rely upon in assessing a suspect's condition are at all related to the consumption of alcohol or drugs.

Have you ever:

- Driven slower than the speed limit?
- Decelerated quickly after seeing a police car in your rear-view mirror?
- Worn shoes (like high heels) that make it difficult to walk heel-to-toe for nine steps in a straight line?
- Used a breath mint?

These very normal actions taken by people every day are among the common ways in which law officers are trained to spot impaired drivers.

Do you have allergies or an eye condition that causes your eyes to occasionally be blood-shot? Have you ever shed a few tears at a particularly emotional movie then driven home? Don't get stopped by the police, because you may be arrested for a DUI.

When you find yourself being questioned by the boss or another figure in authority, do you become confused and fumble your answers? Do you have a medical condition such as ET, Essential Tremor, which causes your hands to shake? Whatever you do, don't get pulled over by police after dark. As far as the police are concerned, you will not be able to pass a roadside test, and you are likely to be arrested for a DUI.

Do you suffer from Gastroesophageal Reflux Disease – that particularly nasty condition in which your stomach contents occasionally rise into your throat? That very occurrence can send the results of your breathalyzer test soaring so quickly and so dramatically, that you'll be under arrest faster than you can say, "heartburn."

Among the following chapters you will learn that in at least one state, the machinery used to test the amount of alcohol in a suspect's breath and blood, is so old and obsolete that parts for the machines are no longer even available – the machines are not just out of warranty, they are no longer manufactured. Can the "scientific" evidence delivered by these arcane devices be sufficient to put citizens into jail? Yes. It happens every day in Washington State.

In a society rightly concerned with the safety of its members, tough DUI laws are welcome safeguards. What is less welcome is the growing pressure for law enforcement to seek and arrest drunk drivers that has become so intense and so very well-funded that "drunk hunting," in some jurisdictions, consumes the lion's share of law enforcement's attention and resources. One might even go so far as to call the effort a budding Witch Hunt.

With the growing influence of the "anti-alcohol" lobby embodied by well-meaning groups like Mothers Against Drunk Driving; money, power, and politics are the fuels for this particular juggernaut. Stricter laws proliferate. Money is made available for MORE dragnets in which to snare the unwary. Games of "who can catch the most drunks" are undertaken in police locker rooms across the country and Joe Public, who was merely trying to set his cruise control when he swerved slightly, finds himself looking for a lawyer.

Unfortunately, it is the liberty of individual citizens that is at stake. The lives and reputations of good citizens crumble under the weight of unfounded accusations and science so fuzzy you could knit a sweater with it.

In A Cup of Coffee With 10 Of The Top DUI Attorneys In The United States, you will find tools to protect yourself and your family from not just the perils of the courtroom – although there is invaluable advice on that front as well – but also how to save yourselves from the paralyzing shame of being convicted. You could be forced to install and use Ignition Interlock Devices in every car you own or might drive, which makes it impossible to start the vehicle until the device has been blown into by the driver and the alcohol content found to be zero. (With his prom-dressed girlfriend in the seat beside him, should Junior really be forced to blow into an IID before he can start the car his mother or father drives? If you're convicted, it may well be part of your punishment. Junior's budding self-esteem, or your wife's suddenly plummeting real estate sales are just collateral damage in the eyes of an overzealous prosecutor.)

Here you'll find answers to questions like these:

- How can I afford to pay a lawyer to defend me?

- What should I say to the arresting officer when he asks if I've been drinking?

- Can I refuse to take a breath test? What happens if I do?

- How can I afford to pay the fines when I cannot even drive myself to work?

- Should I just accept a plea bargain?

- What if they didn't read me my Miranda Rights?

- What are the collateral consequences and how can I minimize them?

You will find, within the pages of this book, answers to these and other questions. You will learn about courtroom strategies used across the country by some of the most prominent DUI Defense Attorneys in the Nation. These same advocates will tell you what to look for in a lawyer, and how to spot a bad one. When, precisely, to ask for an attorney, and if and when honesty really is the best policy.

Should you submit to field sobriety tests at all? Not all top-notch lawyers agree upon this and other key questions around the concept of "implied consent." The consequences associated with refusals vary from state to state; nevertheless, it pays to be prepared to react appropriately should you ever be invited to participate in such a test alongside a busy freeway. Even if you have studied for these tests, you may not pass them. The weather, highway traffic, the very shoes you are wearing, and your own physical condition (quite apart from your alcohol level) can ensure that you will be deemed to be impaired by the officer in charge. You could then be cuffed and stuffed into that waiting police cruiser and on your way to a lifetime of being a known offender. Do yourself the favor of weighing the consequences yourself before you are asked to walk that invisible line. If you drive an automobile, it pays to be proactive.

Perhaps the least reliable law enforcement impairment-measurement tool is the uniformed police officer himself. Before you put the key in the ignition again, learn the 24 "clues" officers may use to determine whether or not you are likely an impaired driver. Understand that if you are at all nervous or intimidated, in the minutes after a stop, the officer's subjective "impressions" of your behavior are likely to show up in his police report as evidence of your intoxication. An officer's subjective opinions and his fallible sense of smell could land you in jail in a heartbeat. This could be your fate even if the "overpowering smell of alcohol" in your car belongs to your

Uncle Fred who called you for a ride home from the poker game. The breath mint in your mouth might just seal the deal.

Because we humans are trained, from an early age, to step up to the proverbial plate and accept the consequences of our misdeeds, many drivers automatically assume that they are guilty of DWI the moment they are pulled over. If they did have a drink or two, they seem compelled to confess their guilt and accept the consequences even though the chances are very good that they are not at all impaired. They throw themselves upon the mercy of the court in spite of the fact that the tools law enforcement relies upon to determine sobriety and the haphazard application of field sobriety tests are highly un-reliable. Incredibly, many people who find themselves charged with driving while impaired don't even take advantage of the many protected rights written into the Constitution to shield citizens from illegal searches, and self-incrimination. Then, to make matters much worse, many people fail to retain a lawyer to help them safeguard their right to equal protection under the law. Those people often regret the decision to accept their conviction meekly for the rest of their lives. The record of your arrest is very, very public and will follow you all the days of your life if it isn't handled by a knowledgeable, experienced DUI defense attorney.

You need not be a problem drinker to read this book. As a matter of fact, if you do frequently drive while impaired, you might be disappointed to learn that the lawyers whose chapters lie within are most interested in getting you off the streets. They are unanimously in favor of driving only when you are sober. Nevertheless, because even the president of the Temperance League can find himself at the side of the highway awash in blinking blue lights, this is a book for anybody who drives.

If forewarned is forearmed, this book is your arsenal. A Cup of Coffee With 10 Of The Top DUI Attorneys In The United States will arm you with everything you'll need know and do if you are ever pulled over by the police and charged with a DUI.

Randy Van Ittersum
Host & Founder – Business Leader Spotlight Show

1

THE BIG NET

by Hunter Biederman, Esq.

Hunter Biederman, Esq.
Law Offices of Biederman & Burleson, PLLC
Frisco, Texas
www.dwifrisco.com

Hunter Biederman is a trial attorney who focuses his practice on DWI defense. As a former Assistant District Attorney in Collin County, he has handled hundreds of DWI cases from the side of a prosecutor. He also has handled DWI 2nd's, Felony DWIs, Intoxication Assault, and even Intoxication Manslaughter cases which very few attorneys have ever handled.

In addition, he was recently named a Super Lawyers Rising Star by Super Lawyers magazine and awarded the prestigious "2012 Litigator of the Year Award" presented by the Collin County Bench Bar Foundation.

He has received training in Standardized Field Sobriety Testing, Intoxilyzer 5000, and Gas Chromatography from world-famous scientists at Axion Laboratories in Chicago, IL.

THE BIG NET

If you read the local newspapers, you've probably noticed that there seems to be a marked increase in arrests for driving while intoxicated (DWI). I don't believe that there are more people driving intoxicated, necessarily. I believe that there are simply more arrests being made. Whether or not these are legitimate arrests depends upon many factors, but the fact is, thanks to an increase in the lobbying efforts on the part of groups such as Mothers Against Drunk Drivers, there is simply more funding available to enable law enforcement to cast a wider net. Of course, when they do, they catch more people who have been drinking and driving. Here in Texas, where I practice, it's still legal to drink and drive. What is against the law is driving when you're intoxicated, which is not always an easy condition to prove.

First of all, understand that DWI laws are good laws. The laws exist for very important reasons. You don't have to search long to find somebody who was hurt or killed by a drunk driver. The laws are there to prevent tragedies. The problem is that it's become a very potent hot-button issue, and people who get elected to the legislature have a difficult time saying no to the lobbyists who want stiffer laws and penalties.

There are promises that every politician makes; foremost among them is the promise that he or she will be tough on crime. Nobody wants to be soft on crime, particularly when the law involves child molesters, perpetrators of domestic violence, and, the one we see the most often in our practice, those people who are accused of driving while intoxicated. Any time there's a bill out there, everybody wants to be tough about the law and tougher still on the offenders, whether they prey sexually on innocent children, beat their wives, or point a two-ton hunk of metal traveling at great speed at other drivers and pedestrians. So, when funding becomes available, it goes in that direction.

The problem is that the net that's being tossed to catch the bad guys today is so big that it's capturing those committing innocent behavior along with those committing guilty behavior. The harshness of the laws along with the increase in the funding to enforce the mandate makes it easier for law enforcement to search out and punish intoxicated drivers.

For example, in Texas, there is a program called the Specialized Traffic Enforcement Program (STEP). This program provides extra funding for police departments in order to catch intoxicated drivers. This special grant funding enables the department to add officers and/or add overtime hours in order for the police to spend more time patrolling the streets, looking for people who might be driving while intoxicated. Again, that's not a bad thing, unless they are arresting people who are not intoxicated. Unfortunately, that happens far too frequently.

Through this book, I hope we can help some of those people understand the law a little better and know what to do if they are arrested, and they just might be, because this can happen to literally anyone.

UNDERSTANDING THE CHARGES

I practice law in Texas, and my advice is specific to my state. That being said, your state's laws are probably not entirely different. In Texas, driving while intoxicated means that the subject of the arrest is operating a motor vehicle in a public place while not having the normal use of their mental faculties, the normal use of their physical faculties, or while having an alcohol concentration above 0.08.

You often hear two terms when you're speaking of driving while impaired: driving under the influence and driving while intoxicated. In most states, DUI is what we call DWI in Texas. Charges for a DWI in Texas can be brought against anybody of any age. In Texas, if you're over 21, you're allowed to have consumed alcohol and operate a motor vehicle so long as you're not intoxicated.

For minors, there are different rules. In Texas, we have a second law called driving under the influence of alcohol (DUI) that applies only to minors. In our state, we have a zero tolerance policy when it comes to minors. They may not have any alcohol in their system and operate a motor vehicle. To be clear here; only a minor can be charged with DUI, but an adult or minor can be charged with DWI.

THE PENALTIES

A DUI is a lower-level crime than a DWI in Texas. A DUI is a Class C misdemeanor, which means the punishment range includes a maximum of a $500 fine. You cannot be punished by a jail sentence with a DUI. A DWI, on the other hand, is a misdemeanor. In Texas, such a misdemeanor is punishable by up to one year in jail, a fine of up to $4,000, or a term of probation, not to exceed two years.

There are really only two ways to resolve a DWI case. The subject is either going to have to plead guilty or not guilty. If the accused pleads guilty, he hopes he will come to a plea bargain agreement with the state. If he pleads not guilty, he's essentially saying he wants to have a trial.

In the case of a DWI, we rarely see the full 180 days jail time imposed. Instead, we expect to see some sort of probationary period, usually one to two years. While somebody's on probation, he or she is going to have to fulfill certain conditions as well:

1. He will be required to meet with a probation officer every month who will monitor him and make sure that he's doing everything he's supposed to do.

2. He will be obliged to attend certain classes and courses that are all required by law in Texas. For example, there's a DWI education class that's conducted by Mothers Against Drunk Driving.

3. He will also be required to take part in a Victim Impact Panel. This is another educational program put on by Mothers Against Drunk Driving. This is a panel discussion that usually includes alcohol or substance

abuse treatment providers, victims of intoxicated drivers, or their families. Often, they will also bring in somebody who hurt or killed somebody as a part of a DWI case to participate on the panel, as well.

4. He will be required to perform community service as part of a DWI conviction. That service can involve picking up trash on the side of the road, working in shelters, or anything in between.

5. He will be required to submit to a Substance Abuse Evaluation and any conditions it imposes.

6. He will be forced to pay a fine. The fine for a DWI ranges anywhere from no fine up to $2,000. In Collin County, where I practice, we usually see fines in the neighborhood of $500 to $800. Invariably, there will be court costs to pay. Those costs will vary from county to county. In our county, we see court costs around $400.

Those are absolutes and they are almost entirely unavoidable. There are also other conditions that may be imposed, but are not mandatory. One of them is jail as a condition of probation. Even though someone is being placed on probation, he can also be sent to jail as a condition of his probation for as many as 30 days. We see this most often in egregious cases: for example, a second offense or higher, or if somebody was injured.

THE IGNITION INTERLOCK DEVICE (IID)

Another condition that can be imposed is the ignition interlock device (IID) or deep lung device, as it is sometimes called. This is a mechanical device that the court requires an offender to install on his car. Before the device will allow the vehicle to start, the driver must blow into it so that it can detect if there is any alcohol present in his/her system. The offender must install this device on any car he/she drives, and it must stay installed until the expiration of the probationary period.

These devices can be extremely burdensome to many people. They can be a great deterrent to driving intoxicated; obviously, they can stop an intoxicated driver from driving. However, these same devices are humiliating to the convicted driver and can cause the loss of jobs in many professions.

Although being on probation, the fines, and the conditions of probation are bad, for most of our clients, the worst penalty associated with a DWI conviction is the fact that this conviction will stay on their record forever. That means that in the future, if you're applying for a promising new job, a mortgage loan, or hoping to be admitted to an Ivy League college, there will be your DWI conviction rearing its ugly head. There's no way to ever get a DWI conviction off of your record.

LICENSE SUSPENSION

A DWI in Texas can also carry with it a driver's license suspension. This suspension can be for up to two years and can be very onerous. Fortunately, Texas allows for occupational driver's licenses, or ODLs. An ODL will allow you to drive to and from work, school, pick up the kids, go to the grocery store, and religious worship. Texas allows for up to twelve hours of driving in a 24-hour period.

In Texas, when it comes to refusing a breath or blood test, a license suspension is not automatic, but, rather, you can request a license suspension hearing. This is a golden opportunity for a good DWI attorney to learn more about the criminal case. This is his opportunity to cross-examine the police officer to find out how much he knows, why he stopped that particular person, and what his experience is with DWI. Is this his first arrest ever? Is it the 50th arrest in his career? This hearing helps the attorney find out a little bit about the officer's background. Has he been a police officer for many years, is this is his first time on the job, or has he been a police officer in other jurisdictions, where he might have done things differently?

It's the opportunity to find out what clues of intoxication the officer thinks he saw, so the attorney can get clues of reasons why he arrested the client. It's also going to be an opportunity to talk to the officer a little bit about the breath or blood test, if it was done. Did he see how the sample was obtained? Did he see whether or not the accused's arm was wiped with alcohol beforehand? When it's all said and done, the attorney can get a transcript from those hearings to use down the road at trial. This gives him the chance to box the officer into a story he cannot change later on.

The very best thing about these hearings in Texas is that there are no state prosecutors present. There are only attorneys from Department of Public Safety, whose main focus is to try to have the driver's license suspended. The DWI attorney is more concerned about whether or not that person's going to be actually convicted of the DWI in the criminal case. So there is a dual purpose of trying to win in order to keep the client's license from being suspended, and giving the client a better chance at winning his criminal case at trial.

WHY RETAIN A LAWYER?

Being convicted of DWI in Texas can cost you your license, a significant amount of money, and even your freedom. The best plan is never to be convicted. That's where a good lawyer comes into play.

It is obvious: having a drunk driving conviction is a bad plan. I understand that there can be circumstances that make you pause before picking up the phone to find a defense attorney. You may think, "I'm guilty," because you failed the field sobriety test or your blood alcohol test. If you don't take anything else away from what I have to say in this book, understand this: *You are only guilty when the court says you are guilty, and not a minute before.* Sobriety tests can be administered incorrectly. Machines used in testing breath and blood can be wrong. Another chapter will discuss this in more detail, but first let me urge you not to go to court alone.

Granted, if you've been arrested and charged, the state will try very hard to prove that you're guilty, but there are successful defenses to drunk driving charges. You probably don't know what they are, but a good defense lawyer does. There's not much point in helping the state prove you're guilty.

First of all, understand that an attorney's job isn't only to help his client escape a charge, but also to make sure that there's a fair punishment when punishment is necessary. If you're going to plead guilty, an attorney who is seasoned in this particular area is going to know what the appropriate punishment is, as opposed to somebody that hasn't been there before. There are a wide range of punishments for DWI: anywhere from up to one year in jail for a DWI first conviction all the way down to a much smaller sentence, such as either a 72-hour hold in jail or probation. Making sure that his client gets a fair punishment is as much a part of a lawyer's job as defending him/her in the first place. Even if he is pleading guilty in a case, an attorney must do everything he can to make sure that the client gets the least amount of punishment that the case calls for.

When you hire an attorney to help you, they will be certain that the fines are negotiated downward and the probationary conditions are as minimally burdensome as possible. The law doesn't make an ignition interlock device an absolute requirement. This can be, as discussed earlier, particularly humiliating and degrading in these cases. If you have an attorney, you might escape this particular punishment altogether. Part of what an attorney must do is ensure that the punishment honestly fits the crime.

On the other hand, a plea of not guilty and trial may be called for in your case. In many jurisdictions, including ours, even if someone goes to trial and loses, the client will face virtually the same punishment as would have been imposed if he had pleaded guilty anyway. Basically, you've got nothing to lose either way.

So many of our clients will say, "Look, if I plead guilty, I've got a zero percent of winning. I'm going to be convicted for life. I'm going to have probation, all the classes and courses. If I plead not guilty, I've got a chance of being found not guilty. Even if I lose, I'm looking at virtually the same punishment anyway. I might as well give it a shot."

At this point, you might say, "How can I afford an attorney?" My answer would be, "How could you *not* afford an attorney?" Yes, there will be fees, but a conviction is going to cost you thousands of dollars. All of that cost is followed by a conviction that you will carry with you for the rest of your life. If you think a good DWI attorney is expensive, try hiring a cheap one. Nothing will cost you more in the long run than hiring a cheap lawyer.

There are a myriad of reasons to go to trial on a DWI charge. The first and best reason for people to want to go to trial is they believe they're not guilty. There's no better reason than that. The second best reason could be that we don't think that the state *can* prove them guilty. Justice can't be served if innocent people are convicted, so the state needs to prove that the client was actually operating a motor vehicle while intoxicated. Often the prosecution will have trouble doing that. The burden of proof is on the state of Texas. We don't have to prove you innocent. The prosecution must carry that water. The state will have to carry that burden all throughout the process and the burden never shifts to the defense.

In Texas in particular, there's very little incentive to pleading guilty, because you're usually going to get about the same punishment, or even less punishment afterwards. Other states offer opportunities for you to be able to get the conviction off your records, something called "deferred probation" or "deferred adjudication," but if you're in Texas, you won't have that option. If you plead guilty, you've got that conviction on your record for the rest of your life. Our clients see that as overly harsh. They will go to trial in order to have the opportunity to be found not guilty and keep the conviction from following them around forever.

When The Blue Lights Come On

Much of your case will depend upon what happened, how you behave, and the precise details of the testing that may or may not have occurred when you got pulled over. The chapter section will help you defend yourself *before* the charges are filed.

Field Sobriety Testing

There are three standardized field sobriety tests that are approved by the National Highway Traffic Safety Administration, or NHTSA. Notice that we call them "standardized" tests. They are intended to be administered and graded according to a precise protocol. Unfortunately, because we have a growing pool of officers, there is a chance they may not be giving the tests in the standardized manner. There are classes, books, and manuals that teach the officers how to do that. I've actually been to the class. I'm certified in standardized field sobriety testing, the same as the officers are. In fact, I'm actually an instructor in the course. I can teach the course that teaches the police officers how to do the testing. Instructors are required to teach the officers to administer the tests the same way every single time, with no variations. If there are ambiguous instructions, the test results can be compromised. The bottom line is, if the officer isn't giving the instructions correctly, he can't necessarily grade the driver correctly.

The three standardized field sobriety tests are:

1. The Horizontal Gaze Nystagmus Test. This is the eye/pen test that you've probably seen on TV. Here, a police officer waves a pen or light in front of somebody's eyes. They're looking for the involuntary jerking of the eyes. Supposedly, if somebody has had no alcohol

introduced into his system, his eyes are going to track smoothly. Once enough alcohol is introduced into the system, the eyes will no longer track smoothly. What we've found in our practice is that judges and juries really don't lend too much weight to this particular test. As they're watching the videos, they're not able to see the person's eyes, so they're not able to see what the officer actually saw that night.

2. The Walk-and-Turn Test. In this test, you have an imaginary line in front of you. You are told to take nine steps heel-to-toe down the line, turn around, and take nine steps back. The officers are taught to look for eight possible clues of intoxication on the test. They are looking for subjects that can't balance during the instructions, starting too soon, stopping while walking, not touching heel to toe, stepping off the line, using arms for balance, making an improper turn, and taking the wrong number of steps. If the officer sees two or more clues on this test, it's regarded as a failure of the test.

3. The One-Leg Stand Test. In this third standardized test, the subject is instructed to stand on one leg with his/her hands and arms down at his/her sides for thirty seconds. In this test, the officer is looking for four possible clues of intoxication. They are: looking to see if the subject sways while balancing, uses his arms for balance, hops, or puts his foot down. If the subject shows at least two of these clues then they are deemed to have failed this test.

The problem with these last two physical tests is not only the physical limitations that some people might have, but also environmental factors—what kind of shoes they are wearing or a sloping road, for example. Additionally, consider the mental limitations a person might have on the side of the road at 2 A.M., potentially being arrested. For most people, it's a very intimidating situation. While they are trying to follow the officer's instructions, they're also unsettled about the officers around them, the lights, and people who might see them as they are driving past. The last two tests will show false positives for people who look like they might be intoxicated but are simply nervous, or just don't have the same physical abilities of somebody else who might be taking the test.

SHOULD YOU TAKE THE FIELD SOBRIETY TESTS?

In my opinion, if you're stopped by the police in Texas and they smell alcohol on your breath, you're going to jail. Regardless of how well you do on those tests, once you step out of the car, you're going to jail. So the question becomes, "Should I take the test?"

When I'm instructing high school students about drunk driving, I'll actually pick one of the high school kids and one of the parents out and give them the tests in front of everybody.

Almost always, one of them fails the test, even though they haven't been drinking at all. If the officer smells alcohol on your breath, you're still getting arrested. If you refuse to take the tests, you are still going to get arrested. However, if you do refuse to take the tests, it will set up a better case in court. Would I rather have a trial in which a client looks horrible on the test because they can't stand on one leg, or would I rather have a trial in which, on the video, the client says, "Look, officer, I just don't feel comfortable taking these tests on the side of the road. It's nothing against you, but I really just don't want to do them"? I see it as a no-brainer.

Ultimately, and from a lawyer's perspective, I'd certainly rather have the client politely saying "Thanks, but no thanks," to the tests on the video. If somebody's intoxicated, they cannot pass these tests. That much is obvious. One of the reasons why people don't do well on the tests is because they're intoxicated, but there are a million other reasons why people do poorly on those tests. It could be that they're not good at listening to instructions and they've got a short attention span. It could be that they're physically unable to do it. It could be they're nervous, scared, or the weather conditions are nasty and windy, or it could be cold out. Perhaps they have shoes that aren't tied tightly or are wearing high heels, wedges, or flip-flops. That's why I advise my Texas clients not to take these tests. I simply don't have the confidence that those tests are going to be done properly in order to be able to exonerate you if you are not intoxicated and you truly are not guilty. I would much rather you not subject yourself to the testing process, period.

WHAT ABOUT BREATH & BLOOD TESTS?

Courts are becoming looser about the introduction of blood tests in relation to constitutional protections in terms of "search," and many police departments have started to obtain search warrants for people's blood if they have refused a breath or a blood test. What they'll do is write up a search warrant and have it signed by a judge who will sometimes be on stand-by for late hours or weekends. Even if you refuse a breath or blood test, they'll be able to force a needle into your arm. If necessary, they will strap you down to take your blood from you, but that's only upon a judge's warrant. An officer can't do that without a judge's warrant in Texas. The important thing to remember is that you *can* refuse. Then, if they want to produce a warrant, they can, and you will need to comply.

The advantage when somebody refuses a blood test and law enforcement has to obtain a warrant in order to get the blood test is that it makes it more difficult for the prosecutors to get the blood test results into evidence in court. There are extra hurdles they have to jump over before a judge or a jury can hear the results. The prosecution will have to make sure that the warrant was drafted and executed correctly and that there were no violations of the rights of the accused. This makes it more difficult than if somebody were to voluntarily give a sample of his or her breath or blood.

The prosecutor can always try to use your refusal against you in court, saying, "Hey, this person didn't give us a breath sample or a blood sample because they knew they were guilty." This strategy by prosecutors is rarely successful if combated in the correct manner.

When the prosecution tries that strategy, it gives us the opportunity to go over a few reasons why people won't want to give a sample. As far as breath samples go, everybody's heard about breath-test machines and whether or not they work. In court, it's not unusual to hear the story of the guy who has a buddy who is a cop, or another lawyer who told them, "Hey, don't ever take the test," for whatever reason. So certainly, while a refusal can be a tool to use against an individual, it's not always an effective method by the prosecutors. After all, it's common knowledge to refuse a breath test. *Everybody* has heard from *somebody* at one point or another not to take the breath test.

When refusing a blood test, similarly, it is obvious why many people would not want to voluntarily do this. No one wants an invasive medical procedure done against them, especially when some jurisdictions are even allowing police officers to perform the blood draws.

One of the good things about DWI in Texas is that if you are found not guilty in a criminal case, you can have a prior license suspension set aside. Say, for instance, your license was suspended for six months for refusal over a breath or blood test, and you were found not guilty in the criminal case. That license suspension would end as soon as that proof is shown at the DPS. It doesn't work the other direction, however. If you win your license suspension hearing, you don't automatically win the criminal case, but again, there could be good pieces of information that the attorney will learn in order to try to assist you in that criminal trial.

Similarly, it's going to make the state's case harder if they don't have a breath or a blood test in the case. The police department will not always be able to obtain a search warrant for blood if someone refuses a chemical test. So, while the ramifications on your license could be potentially worse, this is setting you up to try to keep that criminal conviction from going on your record for the rest of your life (and potentially having the license suspension set aside at a later date). For most people, that's going to be their main goal. So, not only is it going to help you if you might have had a blood alcohol content (BAC) of over 0.08, it's going to help you if you would have been under that. It's also possible that the chemical test isn't going to be done properly and it would show a false positive or inflated score, making your case harder to win.

HINDSIGHT

What if, as you pick up this book, you have already been arrested and voluntarily taken a chemical test?

Many people assume that if they volunteered a breath or blood test that their proverbial goose is cooked, and there's no chance to ever win their case. Over the years, we have learned this from judges and juries who have found our clients not guilty: that's simply not the case. The truth is, there is much more to this testing than the resulting numbers.

First of all, in Texas, the state must prove that you are intoxicated at the time of driving. Imagine that you blew a 0.10. That is extremely close to the line of 0.08. The state is now going to have to prove that you were over 0.08 *at the time of driving*. Bear in mind that the breath or blood tests usually aren't taken for at least an hour, or sometimes up to three hours after the time that the accused was actually stopped or seen driving. We know through pharmacokinetics that an individual's BAC might have been higher, lower, or the same at the time they were stopped. The state must then engage in retrograde extrapolation. That's a term used for attempting to calculate what your alcohol concentration might have been at the time you were driving.

As you're drinking alcohol, you get more and more intoxicated. When you stop drinking, you become less and less intoxicated. Your blood alcohol content might have been higher, lower, or the same when you were arrested, depending upon the time you had your first drink and when you took your last drink. Then, the state must factor in the time at which you were driving and were pulled over. This calculation might be one way to fight breath or blood test results.

Another way might be to challenge the machine itself. In Texas today, we're using the Intoxilyzer 5000, a machine used in about 20 states. This model isn't even the newest machine; the company that makes the machine has developed and released several machines since the Intoxilyzer 5000 came out. Texas hasn't upgraded to the new machines even though we know that there have been improvements in the technology and accuracy. The point can be made that the state seems too cheap to ensure accurate results. Well-seasoned attorneys know the nuances of these machines and where errors can occur.

We keep two Intoxilyzer 5000's in our office that we use to show our clients where and how things can go wrong. If we need to, we can bring those in during a trial to show a jury what can be wrong about it, as well.

The same goes for blood testing. Blood is tested through a process called gas chromatography. This testing method is used nationwide. If you talk to any scientist, they will tell you that gas chromatography is good science. It's absolutely a positive, good way to test a sample of blood to find out how much ethanol is in that sample. The problem with gas chromatography is in the application of the method.

Unfortunately, in Texas, the samples are not run in independent laboratories, but rather state-funded facilities. We have, over the years, been able to point out to juries that those testing procedures may or may not have been followed in the same manner that an independent scientist would follow at either a hospital or a private laboratory. We might also show that the sample taken from an accused driver, either at the jail or at the hospital, was, in fact, a different sample than was tested at the state facility. It could have been another sample from another driver. We can also question whether or not blanks were being run in between the tests or other safeguards were implemented and followed. If the samples are run one after another, we need to ensure that there was no ethanol carried over from the previously tested sample. It is abundantly clear that an attorney can suggest any one of many problems within the testing process.

THE BIG PICTURE

To summarize, your odds of getting arrested for DWI get better (or worse, depending upon your perspective) all the time. Unless you never consume alcohol, you are increasingly likely to get stopped for DUI/DWI. If you are pulled over and asked to get out of the car, you might as well plan on being arrested. Statistically, that's the case. When that happens, you need a lawyer. Given the penalties, it is unwise to gamble the rest of your life and your reputation on your own knowledge of the law.

Find a lawyer who is well-versed in this kind of case. Pick one who has established himself as a lawyer who knows the law, knows the system in the jurisdiction where your arrest occurred, and one who stays abreast of not just the laws around your constitutional protection from illegal search, but also the science and foibles of blood-alcohol testing machinery.

Finally, in some jurisdictions, your lawyer may suggest that taking the sobriety or chemical tests is a good idea, and cooperation with this testing is something you should absolutely do. In our opinion, and in light of Texas law, we discourage our clients from participating in those tests. We urge you to research and understand the law in your state before you get stopped.

(This content should be used for informational purposes only. It does not create an attorney-client relationship with any reader and should not be construed as legal advice. If you need legal advice, please contact an attorney in your community who can assess the specifics of your situation.)

2

FREE ADVICE
THAT YOU CAN
TAKE TO THE BANK

by Tracey Wood, Esq.

Tracey Wood, Esq.
Tracey Wood & Associates
Madison, Wisconsin
www.attorneytraceywood.com

Attorney Tracey A. Wood, the owner of Tracey Wood &
Associates, is an aggressive criminal defense attorney in
Madison, Wisconsin. She is a repeated recipient of the
distinguishing Wisconsin Super Lawyers Award and recently
was named to the Top 25 Women in Law by Super Lawyers.

Attorney Wood is known throughout the legal community as the
foremost authority on Wisconsin OWI DUI laws. She frequently

serves as a criminal law commentator and legal analyst to local media, a guest speaker at national seminars, and an instructor to DUI or OWI defense attorneys across the United States, most recently for Harvard Law School.

She is the first attorney from Wisconsin ever appointed as a Standardized Field Sobriety Test Instructor, and first Wisconsin attorney to be appointed to the Board of Regents to the National College for DUI Defense held at Harvard Law School. She chairs the Wisconsin Association of Criminal Defense Lawyers Strike Force for the state's largest association of criminal defense lawyers and has previously served as the President of that organization.

FREE ADVICE THAT YOU
CAN TAKE TO THE BANK

If you're reading this book, I must assume that you have either been arrested for driving under the influence of intoxicants or that you know someone who has lived through this experience. For now, if I could say just one thing to you, it would be this: Get an attorney—now.

Below are six reasons it's a good idea to retain an attorney:

1. When people are charged with a DUI (or OWI in Wisconsin,) they are so overwhelmed that they fail to think clearly. "I blew a 0.18. I failed the field sobriety test. I'll just roll over, ignore my constitutional rights, and accept my punishment."

2. Charges often depend entirely upon test results and arrest circumstances. Neither police officers nor testing equipment are infallibly accurate—both make daily mistakes—and a DUI charge can be life-altering.

3. The idea of saving money by not retaining an attorney doesn't include the actual costs of a charge of Operating While Under the Influence of an Intoxicant (OWI) or Operating with a Prohibited Alcohol Concentration (PAC). Costs might range from fees and fines, to insurance premium increases, to payment for treatment, to installing an ignition interlock device on each and every vehicle that you own.

4. A DUI or OWI conviction stays on your very public driving record—for life. Questions about your record may appear at every job interview. Also, some states have a point system: if you accrue too many points on your license for small traffic violations, a DUI or repeat DUI may cause you to permanently lose driving privileges.

5. While state laws differ, the underlying process generally follows standard rules because Federal constraints—your constitutional rights from due process to search and seizure—trump any state legislation. Wherever you are arrested, you are innocent unless and until the court finds you guilty.

6. If the officer fails to take the proper steps according to the letter of the law, your case can be dismissed. It's an attorney's job to know the law and insist that it be followed. You probably shouldn't represent yourself in court, even if—or especially if—you went to law school.

Some Supreme Court rulings may be pertinent to your defense strategy. Since these rulings change the way that the process moves forward from the initial traffic stop, it's terribly important to know legal changes related to your case. Overall, the law is a big, complicated maze. Even highly-educated and well-practiced attorneys can have trouble navigating through it. Trying to wander alone through the maze is foolish.

FINDING A QUALIFIED DUI ATTORNEY

Frankly, the Internet is the easiest way to get a lot of information on qualified attorneys. From my point of view, the following are some mandatory qualifications: membership in the National College for DUI Defense, membership in the state organization for criminal defense lawyers (e.g., Wisconsin Association of Criminal Defense Lawyers), and experience or certification in field sobriety testing. Other helpful bonuses include any scientific training they've had in breath or blood testing, their ability ratings on websites (e.g., Super Lawyers and Avvo), and any of their writings dealing with this area of law. Look for articles, co-authored books, and other publications featuring their names.

After you've done your research and narrowed down the options to a few different people, have a five-minute conversation on the phone with the short-list attorneys. You will know immediately whom you like the best and who you think will do the best job for you. If a lawyer just talks about his qualifications without asking anything about your particular case, he probably won't do a good job for you. You want someone who can listen to what you have to say, offer some suggestions on the way the case might go (given what you said), and then also talk about what he or she's done in the past. Follow your gut.

PENALTIES

People should understand what they're facing with a first offense. In Wisconsin, a conviction for a first offense includes mandatory alcohol rehabilitation treatment along with an automatic six- to nine-month revocation of the driver's license. The fines, called forfeitures on civil cases, begin at about $350. From that base minimum, the fines increase depending upon other factors, such as whether or not there was a minor in the car when you were stopped (this also carries jail as a penalty). Additionally, if you showed either a refusal to comply with testing or a Blood Alcohol Content (BAC) of 0.15 or higher by breath or blood, you will be required to install an ignition interlock device on *every one* of your cars for a period of 12 months. This means an installation on every car registered to the person charged, or to which that person has access and might potentially drive.

There's an initial installation charge for each device, followed by a monthly lease fee for each of the devices. At the end of the sentence, an un-installation fee is required. Depending upon the number of vehicles that you own, this can add up to thousands of dollars. All of these fees constitute a condition of driving after an OWI. If you want to drive, you must comply—period. If the person charged doesn't own a car or doesn't drive, the state waits until the person becomes licensed or actually obtains a car. Then, the state requires that the device be installed on the car. Amazingly, this happens even if five years have passed since the OWI.

Here's what the ignition interlock device (IID) requires from you and everybody else in your family. Any person who gets behind the wheel of one of your cars, from your wife driving the kids to school to your teenaged son on a date, that potential driver must blow into the device to determine that there is no alcohol in his/her system before the car can be started.

Regarding teenage sons, Wisconsin residents should know the rules on underage drinking or drinking prior to age 21. Underage drinking for non-drivers can result in a civil conviction and a driver's license suspension. Many people don't know that if their child gets apprehended for underage drinking, that child's license can also be suspended. It's important to involve an attorney to deal with these cases. If a young person (i.e., under age 21) is found in a car after consuming intoxicants, but not enough to impair his or her driving of a motor vehicle, this is called an absolute sobriety violation; and a conviction carries a mandatory license suspension. If the officer thinks there's enough proof of drunkenness (0.08 or higher BAC), both teens and 21-year-old adults will receive the bigger drunk driving offense consequences.

First offenses incur a range of penalties, but those penalties increase with second and higher offenses. Second and third offenses require jail time between five days to six months. By the fourth offense, if you show a prior conviction within the last five years, then the offense becomes a felony case in which prison can be imposed. Since penalties just get worse from that first offense onward, the best plan is to avoid the first conviction.

Especially after a third conviction, it's absolutely imperative to retain a lawyer. The consequences of not having an attorney, or retaining an attorney who is unfamiliar with the OWI process, could ultimately include imprisonment if there are previous convictions. This happens to many people after their third offense.

INTENT OF PLEA BARGAINING

Plea bargaining means that both sides (i.e., state and defense) get something and lose something. The defense attorney's idea is to get his or her client a lesser conviction, like reckless driving or inattentive driving. The state wants to get a severe sentence along with the drunk driving charge. However, before entering into any plea discussions, motions and facts need to be brought out on issues with the testing and police investigation. In my experience, bargaining won't happen unless the other side thinks there's a chance that it could lose the case. Then, all of a sudden, agreements get a lot more attractive. So I never even approach a prosecutor for a plea bargain until I know how I could potentially win the specific case.

USING YOUR CONSTITUTIONAL ADVANTAGES

It might sound cliché, but you really are innocent unless and until you are proven guilty. In criminal work, and before an OWI conviction, the standard that the state must meet to prove someone's guilt is "beyond a reasonable doubt." Reasonable doubts can be raised based upon officer-related issues (e.g., testing problems or arrest problems) or defendant-related issues, such as whether or not the person drank after driving or was operating on a public highway. Little things can make all the difference in one of these cases.

Ultimately, it is not the defense attorney's job to prove innocence. The defense attorney's job is to raise doubt. For that reason, the sooner we're involved, the better it is for our client. Our office leaves no stone unturned; we look at every facet of the case, starting from the initial traffic stop. We obtain any videos, the initial audio recording with the dispatch officer, and any motions that might be filed. We're reviewing all of the evidence from the beginning in order to keep our defense as strong as possible.

At our firm, we are trained and qualified to administer field sobriety tests, which is one of our firm's excellent advantages. I'm an actual instructor of field sobriety testing, so I've gone through everything that police officers go through in training and have the training that the top police instructors have. When someone says that an officer is incorrectly administering a field sobriety test, perhaps by counting certain clues against the arrestee that shouldn't be considered, I can point immediately to the officer's errors. Through my training, I have the advantage of knowing precisely what he's doing wrong.

Let's assume that there was a valid stop for speeding. Generally, the officer is first approaching the car to classify the odor of intoxicants: mild, moderate, or strong. If he establishes that there is an odor of intoxicants, the next step would almost always be to establish whether or not the driver has observable impairment: slurred speech, fumbling for his driver's license, or inability to adequately answer questions.

In many police reports, I often see notes about "bloodshot" or "glassy eyes". One study submitted to the National Highway Traffic Safety Administration (NHTSA), the agency that trains all officers in the administration of sobriety testing, states that bloodshot eyes are no longer considered foolproof indicators of intoxication. People can display red or glassy eyes for a myriad of reasons: allergies, fatigue, smoking, or exposure to a *smoky bar*.[1] In a police report, if bloodshot or glassy eyes are given as a reason for continued detention, I immediately want to review the material, because officers should no longer consider this as a legitimate indicator of intoxication.

If an officer sees enough to justify a continued detention or believes that there's enough evidence for field sobriety testing, he'll ask the person to exit the car. (Currently, some debate in Wisconsin law centers on the question of adequate requirements or precursors for field sobriety testing. The odor of intoxicants alone is not enough because people are still allowed to drink and drive. They just can't drink and show a BAC over a certain limit.) The officer will watch to spot certain behaviors from the subject, from mechanical ability and coordination (e.g., finger dexterity or stumbling and whether or not the person can open the car door without help) to speech pattern problems.

A good OWI defense attorney should have expertise in reading records that often remain behind the scenes, such as mechanical breath and blood testing records. Maintenance records and the procedures for breath and blood testing at the time of the arrest, can provide priceless information for a defense attorney. If a lawyer can't see potential sources of error in the documents, then he is simply taking the data as gospel truth. The data provided by those machines is not always accurate.

The experts who maintain these testing machines would say they are subject to a margin of error between 0.005 and 0.01 for breath, and blood tests are not one hundred percent accurate. Many things can adversely impact those tests. If the subject suffers from gastroesophageal reflux disease (GERD), that fairly common condition could artificially inflate the breath test because alcohol-rich vapors are moving from the stomach into that machine. Our machines in Wisconsin turn off the machine's "slope detector" function, which adjusts for differences between alcohol in the lungs and bloodstream from alcohol in the mouth. Without the "slope detector" function, the readings in the breath test machine (called the Intoximeter) can be seriously inaccurate, so any Wisconsin reading should be suspect.

Also, breath test machines are made out of parts of other machines throughout the country. All of the computer documentation goes through the Chemical Test Section in Madison. Across the entire state, every single breath test result taken on a machine called the Intoximeter (EC/IR II) is noted and documented through a facility in Madison. Technicians check each machine for any errors and determine the types of maintenance that have been done on the machines. After checking the machines' records, our attorneys often find that many of those units have been taken out of service or are arriving for maintenance because they're experiencing some issues or inaccuracies. Breath test cases can be a lot of fun for the defense attorney because errors can occur in so many areas.

These days, an increasing number of police agencies are using blood testing over the breathalyzer, because they feel that blood tests are more reliable. To stay on top of the testing techniques, attorneys in our practice get the same training as the chemists in the state of Wisconsin for administering and reading blood tests. So, we know that there are inherent problems in blood testing. We do a form of testing called "gas chromatography". With the proper scientific training, we're able to see the rates of error. We're also able to see if other compounds are being mistakenly presented as alcohol in the blood. For example, if a person's job exposes him to certain chemicals, those chemicals can appear on the machine with a pattern similar to ethanol, which can artificially inflate the alcohol level.

In my estimation, it's important in all areas of OWI defense to know as much or more than the police, the chemist, and the

41

experts on the other side. In the field of scientific evidence, the defense attorney definitely wants to know more than the prosecutor. Many people, including the prosecutor, simply accept whatever is offered by the test results, but there is entirely too much human error within those test results. It's important for our firm, as well as other lawyers, to learn that fact and not just blindly believe the box when it spits out a test result.

This brings us back to the misguided client who comes in and says, "Hey, I blew two times over the limit," or, "I tested two times over the limit. I'm obviously guilty." This is not necessarily true. Our attorneys have won many cases in which people showed alcohol levels up to two or three times the legal limit due to problems with the analysis of the breath or blood.

Frankly, the more we fight, the more we earn dispositions that other attorneys fail to reach. I receive a lot of amendments or reductions to various charges made against my clients because prosecutors eventually understand that we have done our homework—we are totally prepared to go to trial and argue motions. Further, we're doing things in a way that other people haven't even considered, which can be exhausting for the other side.

DRIVING AND DRUGS

In the state of Wisconsin, another big area of prosecution is titled "driving while under the influence of a controlled substance". Essentially, as I've taught in seminars for other defense lawyers, it's a drunk driving charge but with drugs in someone's system as opposed to ethanol. First of all, Tetrahydrocannabinol (THC)—the principle psychoactive component of the cannabis or marijuana plant—is a prohibited substance. If a detectable amount of THC is found in your blood, it's automatically presumed that your test result will be evidence of your guilt of operating while under the influence of a controlled substance.

Lawyers need to understand the difference between a detectable and an undetectable level. A good lawyer can point out that drug metabolites, which can be markers for drug use, are inactive ingredients of THC. These are insufficient evidence for a conviction for operating while under the influence of a controlled substance.

Also, prescription drug violations and prosecutions are becoming much more common. If a person is stopped for suspected alcohol use and only shows a very small amount of ethanol (or none), the officer will examine the blood for drugs in the system. There may be a combination of prescription drugs in that person's system, some of which may interact badly with alcohol (e.g., Lorazepam). Somebody on the state payroll will say, "That obviously caused impairment so we're going to prosecute!"

The problem with these kinds of prosecutions—which is the best part for the savvy defense attorney—is that nobody knows an individual's appropriate level of medication except that individual and his own doctor. So, no chemist can say, "This is outside the therapeutic level, and that person is obviously too impaired to operate a motor vehicle," unless he or she knows or has done a controlled study on that individual who took that specific level of drugs.

Also, there's no automatic prohibition against using intoxicants with medicines, though the prescription bottle caveat often warns against taking alcohol along with the medication "until you know how it will affect you". After a person has taken a medication for a long time and knows how it will affect him, unless the doctor forbids it, a reasonable amount of alcohol won't have any significant effect. Unless you show visible signs of obvious impairment, such as bad driving or stumbling while walking, impairment can't automatically be assumed from ingestion of a prescription medication mixture.

Prescriptions and over-the-counter medications present a completely new set of problems since, with conditions like diabetes, your driving might be impaired if you forget to take your medication. In the future, people who must take medication for severe allergies may be charged with a DUI. Lawyers should not simply say, "This person's been charged, and drugs were found in his system, so he's automatically guilty." These cases can be won.

REFUSALS AND IMPLIED CONSENT

When I'm asked if a person should submit to a breathalyzer or other tests after he is stopped, I generally say, "Yes, do the test." However, the legality of the arrest and the testing request are important, because the arrest itself can be the key to acquittal.

First of all, the arrest must be valid and must be supported by probable cause. Just to pull the vehicle over, the officer must have a reasonable suspicion that the driver was specifically operating under the influence of an intoxicant or committing a crime. Per the Supreme Court standard of Terry vs Ohio, reasonable suspicion is more than the officers' hunch. Reasonable suspicion includes specific particulars of the actual crime in occurrence for a judge to affirm the stop as valid— especially in a possible suppression hearing. Second, the arrest must be valid and supported by probable cause. Third, before a breath or blood test may be requested by the officer, the officer is required to read a form called "Informing the Accused". This form essentially tells the driver, "We have the right to take your breath or blood, and in return for that, you get certain privileges." When you sift through all the language, this is what it means: "If you don't submit to this test, your license is subject to revocation."

Let's imagine that someone is arrested for OWI by the police. The officer reads the necessary form, telling the driver that his license will be revoked if he doesn't submit to a breath, blood, or urine test. If that person's refusal is upheld in court, meaning the defense attorney is unable to prove to the court that his client had good reason to refuse the test, the person's license will be automatically revoked for a period of time.

As a rule, refusing the breath or blood test is not a great idea unless there's a good defense for that refusal, especially in states like Wisconsin that carry more penalties for refusals than for taking the test. A refusal might be allowed if the driver is from a jurisdiction where refusals don't count against his driver's license in the same way as a drunk driving offense. I have represented out-of-state clients for whom the refusal does not carry consequences as harsh as a drunk driving conviction.

Defenses of refusals are possible for a few reasons, including:

1. Lack of reasonable suspicion for the stop.

2. Lack of probable cause for the arrest.

3. Inability to submit to the breath test machine.

VIOLATIONS OF THE IMPLIED CONSENT LAW

Implied consent violations happen when the officer misstates the driver's rights under the applicable law, or the officers offer to give advice to the driver. This second instance is often the tipping point for an entire case. If a driver asks the officer, "Well, should I take it or not? What will happen to me if I don't take it?" Occasionally, the officers make the mistake of giving their personal opinion on what to do, which is not their job. That officer's job is to read the form, period. We have won many cases because there was either too much or not enough information given by the police officer.

If the officer induced someone to refuse to take the test, or gave advice beyond what he must read word-for-word from the form, then that provides an attorney a defense to the case. If a person wins his refusal case, in all likelihood, he will win the OWI case. If there's a refusal, this may be used at trial as an indication that the driver is conscious of his guilt. Without that refusal evidence—or if there is no refusal evidence and there is no test—there's no evidence to convict the driver. In cases where we've won the refusal, I've never had someone convicted of a drunk driving charge.

ANOTHER TRAP TO AVOID

The defendant also needs to tread carefully in the timing of the request for an attorney. When I taught the refusal section of our annual drunk driving defense seminar, we talked a great deal about the after effects of the defendant exercising his right to counsel too soon. He may tell the officer something like this: "I'll decide whether or not to take this test after I talk to my lawyer."

Unfortunately, the law does not guarantee you an attorney when you're making the decision about taking the test. Nevertheless, the driver's statement of "I want a lawyer" doesn't constitute an automatic refusal. Some officers might say, "We don't have to provide a lawyer to you at this point; that's a refusal." That is absolutely not true.

Also, officers have a good bit of power under the implied consent law, but they also have legal duties to perform, such as informing people of their rights and ensuring that those rights are protected. For instance, informing the subject that he doesn't have a right to an attorney at intoxicant testing time, rather than using that statement against the driver to garner a refusal. The officer's job is to be fair to the subject while finding out whether or not the person is actually operating while under the influence of an intoxicant. Officers should be seeking the truth, not playing a game of "gotcha" in order to get a conviction.

If you're stopped, remember this additional right: under the implied consent law, you have the right to go through a second test at the cost of the police agency. If you prefer to have the choice of the person administering the test, it can be done at your own expense. A second test is one of those due process rights that you can insist upon. The law allows you to get that second test in exchange for your cooperation in taking the first test.

THE CHANGING LEGAL LANDSCAPE

The McNeely Case

In April of 2013, the United States Supreme Court came down with a ruling in the case of *Missouri vs. McNeely*. This ruling held that in DUI blood-draw cases, the police must obtain warrants from magistrates or judges before drawing blood, unless constitutional consent is given. Prior to this time, police were regularly ordering a blood draw without getting a warrant because it was considered an exigency or a time-sensitive situation, since the blood might not show evidence of intoxication if the warrant caused a delay.

The Supreme Court essentially said to law enforcement officials, "That's no longer okay. You need to get a warrant. When you're sticking a needle under someone's skin, that's a search, and searches of citizens in the United States are constitutionally protected." In three recent joint cases, The Wisconsin Supreme Court noted that McNeely also applies in Wisconsin. Our firm argued one of those three cases this last fall.

This is our firm's position:

1. The state of Wisconsin exists within the United States, so McNeely applies.

2. Cases prior to the McNeely decision should not be entitled to good faith. Though the state has argued for pre-McNeely cases to stand as "adjudicated in good faith" since the officers were relying on the old law allowing blood draws without warrants, our firm doesn't agree. Currently, the Wisconsin Supreme Court's position is that good faith does protect officers in pre-McNeely cases.

3. It's the state of Wisconsin's burden to show consent if there's no warrant.

This third point is very interesting. When the officer reads the "Informing the Accused" form to the driver, it essentially says this: "If you don't allow us to take a sample of your breath, blood, and urine, you'll suffer license revocation and other things." Most people assume, along with the state, that consent is given when an arrestee says, "Fine, go ahead and sample my blood or breath; I agreed to it after you've read this form." In our firm's view, this kind of "consent" is simply forced acquiescence to police authority, akin to duress. If somebody holds a gun to your head and says, "Give me your wallet," giving up your wallet isn't really an "agreement" or constitutional consent to give up your property.

Our attorneys argue that *Missouri vs. McNeely* mandates warrants in just about every blood draw. Moreover, it also mandates warrants in breath tests because a breath sample is really a search of the deep alveolar lung air. Therefore, it is as much of a search as any kind of blood test. We're having fun with motions, challenging the way tests have been conducted in Wisconsin for many years. We're also ensuring that warrants are obtained in a constitutional manner.

The Gant Case — Illegal Search

Another ruling that has changed OWI case processing is *Arizona vs. Gant*. Before the Supreme Court ruling in Gant, every time that someone was arrested for drunk driving, the police would automatically search the driver's motor vehicle on the "incident to arrest" theory that assumes a constitutional protection. This theory indicated that the search was necessary because the officer wanted to be sure that the subject wouldn't have access to the car or to the possible contraband inside that vehicle.

After the Supreme Court reviewed the case, they refuted the theory. "Officers, you're not allowed to simply search anyone's car after arrest. If you've handcuffed the suspect in the back of the squad car, the incident to arrest search theory disintegrates." Obviously, once someone is handcuffed or has no access to his car, there's no reason to allow that search without a warrant.

In Wisconsin, it was common for police to search the cars on a basis of "incident to arrest". Those searches resulted in many drug prosecutions. The police would find bottles with alcohol, open cups with alcohol, as well as drug paraphernalia. In their reports on suspects who have been drinking, officers write down that they know they may find evidence of drinking in the car. It's clear that the officers are operating on the idea that they are searching for contraband incident to the arrest, which is impermissible. It's important for every OWI lawyer to watch this carefully. If something was found in that car that might hurt the client's case, then *Arizona vs. Gant* might be applicable. A number of years ago, I wrote an article addressing such illegal searches in the Wisconsin Law Journal.

When the final ruling was issued in the Gant case, the police slowed down on those unconstitutional searches. Lately, I've noticed an increase in the "incident to arrest" searches of those cars. I believe that defense lawyers need to revisit many of these challenges.

Collateral Attack

In 1993, I actually had the first case in Wisconsin in which the issue of collateral attacks was raised. A collateral attack means that if the defendant showed prior criminal OWI offenses on his record, and if the defendant did not have a lawyer and his right to be legally represented was not properly waived, the state can't use an old case against the client to enhance the penalties or generate additional punishment.

Since then, I've worked through a few variations on this situation. In my very first case in which I raised this issue, our client's two out-of-state convictions were being used to charge him for the third offense in Wisconsin. I argued that my client was a first offender for two reasons:

1. There was no proof that he had an attorney in his previous convictions.

2. There was no proof that the law under which he was convicted in those other states was substantially similar to Wisconsin's law.

That turned out to be a winning case for us. The court reversed and said, "You're right, because there is no proof that he had a lawyer or that he waived his right to an attorney, nor any proof that the offense of which he was convicted was similar to ours here in Wisconsin." In the end, my client was found guilty of only a first offense; in Wisconsin, this was a civil offense without jail time. I wrote an article teaching other lawyers how to use that particular defense a few years later. To this day, in Wisconsin, collateral attacks are still a very effective weapon for defense attorneys.

Any time an attorney's client shows prior criminal drunk driving convictions (OWI in this state), he should look at whether or not this defense is applicable. First, attorneys should check on whether or not their clients exercised their constitutional right to retain an attorney in their previous cases. Second, they should learn whether or not that client waived that right to attorney, since an attorney can discover defenses that a client didn't know about. Attorneys can work to mitigate sentencing and might be able to secure an amendment to a different charge. Third, the attorney should file a motion to collaterally attack a prior conviction so that the prior can't be used to beef up or double down on the current sentence.

Appeals

Attorneys uncover many cases in which the defendant should not have gotten a conviction in the first place. For that reason, our firm is well-known for our appellate work in criminal and OWI, or drunk-driving cases. In a first offense case, because it's a civil case, we'll file a civil appeal. In criminal cases, obviously, we file a criminal appeal. When another attorney loses an OWI case, he or she will often refer the case to me in hopes that I can get it reversed on an appellate issue.

In one of our very recent cases, a man had gone to trial and been found guilty. (He had been sitting outside of a bar in an idling car, sleeping.) In light of Wisconsin law, the Court of Appeals reversed the finding, because there was insufficient proof that the defendant was operating a motor vehicle. That decision was a little surprising, because the law has been leaning to defining "operation" in this way: if you could have manipulated any controls in the motor vehicle, you were in operation of that vehicle. Ultimately, the Court of Appeals ruled that there should be strong proof that the controls were actually manipulated by that individual in order for a conviction on a drunk driving case.

Since this man held a Commercial Driver's License (CDL) for work, the conviction would have included an automatic one-year disqualification on the first offense. (Subsequent convictions would mean that he would have been forever barred from holding a CDL.) We were able to convince the prosecution to give us an amendment to a reckless driving charge, so he was able to save his regular and commercial driver's licenses.

DEALING WITH THE TRAUMA

Your Own...

An OWI or a DUI can be the worst thing that's ever happened to some of my clients. In my firm, we represent celebrities, judges, and political figures, as well as regular people who go to PTA meetings and Little League games. We also represent real people like doctors, lawyers, and teachers. This kind of charge crosses all levels of society. The trauma of being arrested is bad enough for them, but then they imagine what else can come down the pike if they are found guilty—like having to blow into an IID every time before starting the car at the grocery store or at the golf course. If alcohol treatment is necessary, we talk about it with our clients. We want to make sure that the behavior doesn't get repeated, but also that the consequences are not onerous for our clients. That way, it becomes just a blip as opposed to a life-changing event.

People hire us because of our level of expertise and experience, the results that we're known for getting, and the fact that we do everything possible on every single one of our cases. For the benefit of our clients, we will find any possible motion that can be brought up regarding the stop, the arrest, destruction of evidence (such as a video), or any problems with the breath test machine or blood test. I don't know many other attorneys who actually have the same level of expertise as our firm does in motion practice, trial practice, and scientific knowledge. Our clients spend a lot of money on their defense. We are expensive, but the clients are happy at the end of the defense.

...And Someone Else's

Very often, attorneys who handle this kind of work get polarized, and become victims in their own right. The case becomes a fight between Mothers Against Drunk Driving and the lawyers who "try to get the perpetrator of the crime off the hook."

Our legal system in the United States is the fairest on the planet. Since everyone is considered innocent until legally proven otherwise, the accused has the unequivocal right to the best possible defense. Our country is founded on those principles, and lawyers are making that system work as it was meant to work. So, until there is an end to drunk driving, there will be a need for somebody to represent the accused. I would be delighted to find another career because I'm not needed anymore. Sadly, that just won't happen.

Personally, I have the advantage of having spent a long time dealing with some horrible cases and meeting some wonderful people whose lives have been affected by this crime. I was invited to help set up the Victim Impact Panels in my county, in which people who have lost loved ones due to drunk driving talk to offenders and work through the difficulties and the impact that this event has had on their lives. This is healing for the victims and a great way to help offenders not reoffend.

It is very helpful for people who have been charged with these offenses to hear that their actions have caused devastating consequences for other people. I believe, and anecdotal evidence suggests, that this sort of program can help to lessen the problem of recidivism.

Many people on that panel were representatives of Mothers Against Drunk Driving. Over time, we've gotten to the point where we both respect each other. Working with these groups and seeing the impact of people's decisions makes everyone face the question: "What will it take to reduce drunk driving or drunk driving recidivism?"

Jail time doesn't seem to help, but treatment does appear to have an impact. I believe it's very important to have more treatment options available for people to make sure that, if they get one drunk driving conviction, it never happens again.

Some of these cases are just so sad. In my job, I sometimes have the task of standing in a courtroom representing someone in an OWI homicide case. In that same room is somebody who has lost a loved one, such as a child or a husband, and the last thing that the mother or wife wants to hear from the attorney is that the accused did nothing wrong. On the other hand, I have to do my part to keep this justice system operating in the way that the founders planned it.

In some hearings, the first thing that I do is to walk up to the victim's family and apologize for their loss. I tell them that in anything I do, I promise not to add to their pain. That's a different approach from most other lawyers. Of course, other attorneys tell me, "I wouldn't go up and talk to the victim's family." For me, without fail, it's always something that's been helpful for the case and the victim's family. It costs nothing to be a compassionate human being—even in the courtroom.

I'm also a big advocate and teacher of restorative justice, which is an area of law and a movement that has sparked some recent interest. The term revolves around those who are directly affected by a crime, giving victims an opportunity to have a conversation with the offender about the effect of the tragedy, and share their hurt and their pain. While it's not a means of allowing someone to scream at the other person, if both sides are willing, this process can be helpful to both the offender and to the victim.

I've also come to know that people who lose someone in a horrible accident often don't realize that the at-fault person is a normal person, just like they are. The accused just happened to ingest alcohol before the event took place. In other cases, the person who committed the crime hasn't yet realized the impact of his actions on somebody else. This is a wonderful way to get some humanity back into the system. In the final analysis, this kind of opportunity to see the crime on a human level can lessen recidivism and make everybody feel better about the justice system.

This is the best advice that I can give to my clients and potential clients: this is just a blip in your life. Take care of yourself and your family situation by getting an attorney. If you can't afford me, get somebody that you can afford. Life will get better if you take care of yourself. If you need some alcohol treatment, have your lawyer find someone who can help. Move on with your life and let your attorney deal with your case. While it is hard, and there will be consequences, the idea is to make the process as painless as possible—and to make sure that it never happens again. I tell people, "I hope you don't come back—you can just send friends."

(This content should be used for informational purposes only. It does not create an attorney-client relationship with any reader and should not be construed as legal advice. If you need legal advice, please contact an attorney in your community who can assess the specifics of your situation.)

_____

References:

[1]"The Detection of DWI at BACs Below 0.10" *U.S. Department of Transport ation National Highway Traffic Safety Administration*, Jack Stuster, PhD, CPE, Project Director, 12 Sep. 1997, http://www.drugdetection.net/NHTSA docs/Stuster Detection of DWI at BAC's below 0.10%25.pdf

3

DIFFERENT
TYPES OF DUIS

by Brian D. Sloan, Esq.

Brian D. Sloan, Esq.
Law Office of Brian Douglas Sloan
Phoenix, Arizona
www.arizdui.com

Attorney Brian Sloan has spent his entire career focused on DUI Defense representation, having represented over 1,900 DUI clients in the past 10+ years and done more than 70 felony trials.

He has written numerous published articles, created legal guides and charts used by attorneys throughout Arizona, trained 1,000+ attorneys on DUI representation at statewide seminars, and has received numerous awards and accolades from legal associations and publications. He is rated 10 out of 10 on AVvo.com; rated 4.9 out of 5.0 on Martindale-Hubbell, and was awarded the 2013 Southwest Rising Star Award by Super Lawyers. He also received the "Top 100 Trial Lawyer" in the nation by the National Trial Lawyers Association.

Mr. Sloan also successfully argued that under the new Daubert Scientific Standard is scientifically unreliable and should result in the Blood Test Results being completely suppressed. This was a significant win for the DUI Defense community. An experienced DUI defense attorney can identify police mistakes, unreliable breath, blood, and urine tests, and other legal issues that often make the difference between successful and unsuccessful results in DUI / Drunk Driving case.

DIFFERENT TYPES OF DUIS

There are several different types of DUIs in Arizona, some of which are Felony charges and some of which are Misdemeanors.

In Arizona, "Regular DUI" is a Misdemeanor offense and alleges that a person was impaired to the slightest degree by alcohol, drugs, medications, vapor releasing substances, or a combination thereof; or has a blood alcohol level above 0.08 but below a 0.15. An "Extreme DUI," a Misdemeanor offense, is defined as a person having a blood alcohol level at or above 0.15, but below a 0.20. A "Super Extreme DUI," a Misdemeanor offense, is defined as a person having a blood alcohol level at or above 0.20.

A Misdemeanor DUI can become a Felony charge if one of the following applies: 1) The person's license or privilege to drive was suspended, revoked, cancelled, refused, or restricted; 2) The person had a child under the age of 15 in the vehicle at the time; 3) The person was ordered to have an Ignition Interlock Device placed on any vehicle they operated at the time; or 4) The person has two or more, prior or subsequent, DUI convictions within seven years. What would otherwise be a Misdemeanor DUI can also become a Felony charge if there was an accident where there were injuries or death, or, occasionally, where there is horrific driving.

There is also a separate DUI-like charge that can occur for someone who is under the age of 21 at the time. It is technically not a DUI, but is referred to by Attorneys as Baby DUI. The more proper term is Driving With Alcohol in the Body While Under 21. If convicted of this offense, depending on the person's age, his or her license will likely be suspended for two years, but the driver may be eligible for a restricted license.

There are also DUI charges for those who are impaired by drugs or medications, or those who simply have drugs or medications in their system that are not prescribed or that are not being taken as prescribed.

DUI AND PRESCRIPTION DRUGS

Many people are charged with a DUI simply for taking the prescription medication that they may have been taking for years. For example, let's say that someone commits a traffic violation (like making a wide turn or failing to come to a complete stop at a stop sign), and gets pulled over by a police officer. If the officer has a suspicion that the person is taking drugs or medications, that person could be charged with a DUI, regardless of the length of time that the person had been taking those prescription medications. I have gone to trial with clients who had been taking the same prescription medications for 20 years yet had to go to court to face a DUI charge on the allegation that they were driving impaired, or simply that they had their medication in their system while driving. For Attorneys, those tend to be better cases to take to trial than Alcohol DUIs, since jurors seem to be more understanding of that type of situation. It is more likely that the accused person will be acquitted of the DUI offense, as long as the driving was not horrendous.

However, the accused person must still deal with the stress of getting charged with a DUI, simply for taking medication that had been prescribed. Arizona law allows a person to be charged for Driving Under the Influence of Drugs/Medications in two ways. Under Count 1, the person charged with "driving while impaired to the slightest degree." Under Count 2, the person is charged with "driving while having any drug (or medication) or its metabolite in the system". Under Arizona law, taking a prescription medication as prescribed is a defense to Count 2, but it is not a defense against Count 1. A jury can still find that a person was taking prescription medication as prescribed, yet was impaired to the slightest degree while driving due to taking that prescription medication and is therefore guilty of a DUI.

Charges involving DUI Drugs and DUI Medications are, for the most part, treated the same as a 1st Time Regular DUI. The sentencing range is from one day in jail up to six months in jail. The only exception being that, if someone were to be convicted of a 1st Time DUI Alcohol case, the driver's license would very likely be suspended for 90 days, with the possibility of getting a restricted license for the last 60 days. With a DUI Drugs conviction, the license would be revoked for one year, with no possibility of getting a restricted license.

Unfortunately, in Arizona, Medication DUIs are treated the same as Illegal Drug DUIs. In the eyes of the law, if someone is Driving Under the Influence of meth or cocaine, that is the same as someone Driving under the Influence of Xanax or Ambien, even if that person had a valid prescription for that medication and was taking it as prescribed.

ADMIN PER SE/IMPLIED CONSENT — LICENSE SUSPENSION

In Arizona, when a person is suspected of DUI, they will likely receive what is called an Admin Per Se/Implied Consent Affidavit. This is usually a pink and/or yellow piece of paper. The suspect's license to drive (or privilege to drive) will be suspended for 90 days, simply for being suspected of DUI. However, it may be possible to get a restricted license to drive to/from work/home/school for the final 60 days. This 90-day suspension is usually set to start 15 days after the date of arrest (or date the suspension is served).

It is possible to delay the start of the suspension, but in most cases, it will very likely be inevitable that a person will have to go through the suspension for being suspected of DUI. There are deadlines for requesting a hearing and certain pitfalls to avoid. If handled incorrectly, a person may have to have SR22 High Risk Insurance, where one would not otherwise have to have it.

This is why it is so important to talk to an experienced DUI Defense Lawyer as soon as possible after an arrest, so that you don't lose out on opportunities you may have and don't end up with long-term consequences you may have been able to avoid.

Occasionally, an Admin Per Se/Implied Consent Affidavit is not served on a person at the time of the arrest, but rather a letter will be sent from the Arizona Department of Transportation/Motor Vehicle Division at a later date, once the officer submits the paperwork requesting a suspension. This situation can come with its own pitfalls, including not getting the letter, resulting in one's license being suspended without them even knowing it, or leading to a requirement to have SR22 High Risk Insurance, which can cost a few thousand dollars over the course of a few years.

The Implied Consent is a one-year suspension of one's license or privilege to drive if the person refuses to consent to a blood, breath, or urine test, as requested by the officer, at the time of arrest. It is very likely that this refusal would prompt an officer to get a warrant, and upon that warrant being approved by the judge, the person's license or privilege to drive would be suspended for one year, and the officer will, nonetheless, be able to draw the blood, pursuant to a warrant.

If an Implied Consent one-year suspension goes into effect, it is possible to get a restricted license to drive to/from work/home/school after doing the first 90 days of no driving, as long as the person has an Ignition Interlock Device (IID) installed and has SR22 High Risk Insurance. Note that having an IID installed during this period of time does not count towards any IID requirement that may come with a DUI conviction.

The Admin Per Se suspension and Implied Consent suspension are completely separate from the DUI case itself, which can complicate matters. Since these issues are separate, it is possible for the DUI case to be completely dismissed, or for a Defendant to be acquitted at trial, yet still have to deal with the license suspension for being suspected of DUI or have to deal with the one-year license suspension for refusing the blood draw at the time of arrest.

PUNISHMENTS AND CONSEQUENCES FOR A DUI CONVICTION

DUI laws, punishments, and consequences are constantly changing. It seems not a legislative session goes by without some adjustment to DUI laws.

As of the writing of this book, a 1st Time Regular DUI conviction carries minimum fines and fees of approximately $1,500, with a sentencing range of one day to six months in jail. A person is required to do substance abuse counseling, have an Ignition Interlock Device installed on any vehicle he or she operates (except, possibly, in a DUI Drugs case, but only if handled correctly), and may have to pay for their day(s) in jail. Up to five years of probation can be ordered, and a person will have to do Traffic Survival School. A conviction can also come with SR22 High Risk Insurance and Community Restitution (Community Service).

For a 1st Time Extreme DUI conviction—having a blood alcohol content between .150 and .199—the sentencing range is 30 days to six months in jail, and minimum fines and fees of approximately $2,800. A person is required to do substance abuse counseling, have an Ignition Interlock Device, and may have to pay for their days in jail. Up to five years of probation can be ordered, and a person will have to do Traffic Survival

School. A conviction can also come with SR22 High Risk Insurance and Community Restitution (Community Service).

In Arizona law, there is also a charge that Attorneys refer to as a "1st Time Super Extreme DUI"—having a blood alcohol content at or above a .200—which carries minimum fines and fees of approximately $3,200, with a sentencing range of 45 days to six months in jail. A person is required to do substance abuse counseling, have an Ignition Interlock Device, and may have to pay for their days in jail. Up to five years of probation can be ordered, and a person will have to do Traffic Survival School. A conviction can also come with SR22 High Risk Insurance and Community Restitution (Community Service).

For a 2nd Time Regular DUI within seven years of any first time DUI offense—if not charged as a Felony—the minimum fines and fees are approximately $3,500, with a sentencing range of 30 days to six months in jail. A person is required to do substance abuse counseling, have an Ignition Interlock Device, and may have to pay for their days in jail. Up to five years of probation can be ordered, and a person will have to do Traffic Survival School. A conviction will also come with SR22 High Risk Insurance and Community Restitution (Community Service), as well as a one year license revocation.

For a 2nd Time Extreme DUI within seven years—if not charged as a Felony—the minimum fines and fees are approximately $3,700, with a sentencing range of 120 days to six months in jail. A person is required to do substance abuse counseling, have an Ignition Interlock Device, and may have to pay for their days in jail. Up to five years of probation can be ordered, and a person will have to do Traffic Survival School. A conviction will also come with SR22 High Risk Insurance and

Community Restitution (Community Service), as well as a one-year license revocation.

For a 2nd Time Super Extreme DUI within seven years—if not charged as a Felony—the minimum fines and fees are approximately $4,600, with a requirement of six months in jail. A person is required to do substance abuse counseling, have an Ignition Interlock Device, and may have to pay for their days in jail. Up to five years of probation can be ordered, and a person will have to do Traffic Survival School. A conviction will also come with SR22 High Risk Insurance and Community Restitution (Community Service), as well as a one-year license revocation.

For a license revocation on all the above 2nd Time DUI Offenses, it can be possible to get a restricted license after doing at least 45 days of no driving at all.

All of the above DUI charges are Misdemeanors. Unfortunately, most people, by the time they get their second DUI, it is charged as a Felony, because there is some other issue associated with the DUI such as, most commonly, a license issue at the time of the stop.

Arizona law does include Aggravated DUIs, which are classified as Class 6 or Class 4 Felonies. A Class 6 Aggravated DUI occurs when someone is driving, or in Actual Physical Control of a vehicle, with a child under the age of 15 in the vehicle, while under the influence of alcohol, drugs, medications, vapor-releasing substances, or a combination thereof. A Class 6 Aggravated DUI charge includes a sentencing range of one day in jail up to two years in prison, at least $4,700 in fines and fees, and a one-year license revocation. A two-year ignition interlock device requirement, alcohol screening and counseling; and SR22 high-risk insurance is also required. There will also be a term of probation up to 10 years, which can be supervised or unsupervised.

There is also, however, a provision in Arizona law, which can allow a judge to decide that it is appropriate to leave the Class 6 Felony as a Designated Felony; an Undesignated Felony, which allows the person to earn a Misdemeanor; or to designate the Felony as a Misdemeanor at the time of sentencing. In the event the Felony is reduced to a Misdemeanor, the person would still have all the terms and conditions of a Class 6 Felony. However, the incident would be deemed a Misdemeanor for all other intents and purposes.

In Arizona, there are several reasons why a person may get charged with an Aggravated DUI as a Class 4 Felony: 1) The person has two or more, prior or subsequent, DUI convictions within seven years of the commission date in the present offense; 2) The person was driving under the influence of alcohol with a suspended, revoked, cancelled, refused, or restricted driver's license or privilege; 3) The person was ordered to have an Ignition Interlock Device on any vehicle they operate at the time that they were stopped for DUI, regardless of whether the device was actually installed on the vehicle or not, and regardless as to whether the substance in the person's system was alcohol, drugs, medications, vapor-releasing substances, or a combination thereof.

A Class 4 Aggravated DUI carries with it a minimum of $4,700 in fines and fees, four months to 3.75 years in the Department of Corrections, alcohol screening and counseling, a one-year driver's license revocation, a two-year Ignition

Interlock Device requirement, and SR22 high-risk insurance. There will also be a term of probation up to 10 years, which can be supervised or unsupervised.

The only sentencing exception for a Class 4 Felony Aggravated DUI is an Aggravated DUI alleging that a person was required to have an Ignition Interlock Device installed at the time of the offense. As of the writing of this chapter, technically the Legislature did not include a required minimum sentence to be imposed for that charge. So, in theory, if convicted of a Class 4 Aggravated DUI—Ignition Interlock Device, a Defendant can receive a sentence of any time from zero days in jail, up to 3.75 years in prison, for being convicted of this offense.

Aggravated DUI convictions, whether Class 6 Felonies or Class 4 Felonies, are forever allegeable, which means that they can always be used against a person as a "Prior Felony Conviction." If someone has a prior Aggravated DUI conviction, and commits *any* other type of Felony offense in the future, that person will be looking at substantially more prison time because of the prior Aggravated DUI conviction, regardless of how old the Aggravated DUI conviction is.

Also, know that all of the above-mentioned Felony sentences represent the potential sentence for a 1st Time Aggravated DUI. Aggravated DUIs with one or more prior felony convictions of any kind, comes with substantially harsher punishments, up to and including the potential for 15 years in prison.

HIRING THE RIGHT ATTORNEY

Regarding hiring an Attorney, I think that the most important piece of advice is this: Do Your Research. The idea of hiring the most expensive Attorney to get the best result is a fallacy. Many expensive Attorneys are not very good. They charge a lot of money because people assume that they are good, because they charge a lot of money.

Not all private Attorneys are equal. Find out which ones focus on DUI Representation. In Arizona, Attorneys are not permitted to say that they "specialize" in DUI Defense, unless they have been confirmed as a Specialist by some sort of oversight committee. Despite the fact that I've spent my entire career in DUI Defense, I cannot say that I "specialize" in DUI defense. Rather, I *focus* my law practice on DUI Defense. It is important to find out who is the best Attorney for your situation, not just who has the best price or who is charging the most. Also know that there are quite a few attorneys out there that claim to "specialize" in DUI defense, but they are doing so in flagrant disregard for Arizona State Bar rules. There are only a few attorneys in the state of Arizona who have actually become DUI Specialists. Research is the key.

There is a website called Avvo.com that rates Attorneys and gives people a lot of information about various Attorneys throughout the nation. One of the most helpful features is a pie chart that shows how much of each Attorney's practice is devoted to certain areas of law. I think that it is a wonderful resource for people to use to view what other Attorneys in the community are saying about a certain Attorney, the testimonials given for the Attorney, and the specific areas of law in which the Attorney practices.

Reading the Attorney's website is another good way to research an Attorney. Many Attorneys can claim to be DUI Lawyers but if you really look at their Avvo profiles, and at their websites, you see that they are not really all that experienced in DUI Defense. Take everything with a grain of salt. You cannot trust everything that you read on the Internet.

Referrals can also be a good source of information about Attorneys, but they should not be the sole factor in deciding whom to hire for your DUI case. I cannot say that I have ever had a referral from a police officer. Usually, if a police officer recommends a Defense Attorney, that Attorney would not likely be the one you want to go with. A good defense Attorney will make a police officer's jobs harder. Police officers want bad Defense Attorneys who will not put up a fight. I have had referrals from past clients, from judges, and from probation officers, but I have never had a referral from a police officer. I think that referrals are great, but they are still not a substitute for doing your own research, to see the kind of work that the Attorney can really provide, and to find the best Attorney for your situation.

I offer a one-hour Free "In-Depth" Consultation. I review my initial thoughts on the case, based on what the potential client tells me about their recollections from the incident. I explain how the process works, what the person is facing, what the likely outcome might be, and any issues that I may see. I give people a lot of information when I meet with them during the Free Consultation. I think that people need to be comfortable with their Attorney. One of the things that I offer to clients, which I do not think is usual for most Attorneys, is my personal cell phone number. Clients can get in touch with me directly. They can text me. They can email me. They can call me if they have any questions about anything. It can be a scary time for them, and when questions come up, you do not want to go through a receptionist or a secretary or wait around for a few hours or days in the hope that the Attorney will get in touch with you. When clients fire their old attorney to hire me, this is one of the biggest benefits that I am complimented on.

I would say that the majority of my clients are first-time offenders. When I am representing a client, I try to make it clear that things just get worse from here. When someone is charged with a 1st Time DUI offense, it is a slap on the wrist, but it is a very hard slap on the wrist. It is meant to teach people to never do it again. Most people, by the time they get their second DUI, are charged with a Felony. The reason why the vast majority of first time DUI offenses are Misdemeanors is to teach someone a lesson, hopefully ensure that they never do it again, and if they do get arrested for DUI again, the potential punishment gets substantially worse.

Being an Attorney is not only about helping people in the present but also about helping them in the future. A good Attorney will help their clients understand the importance of not putting themselves in a position for Felony charges, not putting themselves through the stress of large amounts of jail or prison time, and hopefully not facing a Felony on their permanent record. When I talk to people, I feel that I am not only an Attorney for the present case, but a counselor for the future.

THE MIRANDA WARNING

The famous Miranda Rights actually originated in Arizona. What ended up before the United States Supreme Court as *Miranda v. Arizona* actually traveled through the state court system until it reached the highest court in the land. The United States Supreme Court ruled that people must be advised of their Constitutional Rights when they are arrested. "You have the right to remain silent. Anything you say can and will be used you against you in a court of law. You have the right to be represented by an Attorney. If you cannot afford one, an Attorney will be provided to you at no cost. Do you understand these rights? Will you waive these rights?" That is what Miranda Rights are supposed to be. However, little-by-little, since that United States Supreme Court decision in 1966, our Miranda Rights have been chipped away, to the point where they are almost meaningless.

In 2013, a decision was handed down from the United States Supreme Court holding that, in order for a person to invoke his Constitutional Right to Remain Silent, he must actually tell the officer that he wants to invoke his Right to Remain Silent. It is not enough simply to be silent.

In Arizona, Court of Appeals and Supreme Court cases have come out stating that a person needs to be unambiguous when requesting the right to an Attorney; that an officer need not provide someone his Miranda rights upon being arrested, and needs only to provide Miranda rights if questions are asked in order to elicit inculpatory evidence; and that an officer's failure to provide full Miranda rights, as stated by the United States Supreme Court in 1966, does not necessarily mean that the Miranda warnings that were given will be considered insufficient.

This is very different from situations that people see on television, in which the officer reads the suspect his Miranda Rights the moment the handcuffs are placed on that person's wrists. Unfortunately, rarely does that actually happen, at least in the state of Arizona. Oftentimes, an officer will hold off on reading Miranda Rights until after the administration of the blood, breath, or urine test; and it is usually one of the last things that the officer will do, prior to releasing the suspect.

The current case law in Arizona holds that if an officer is going to ask someone questions intended to elicit inculpatory evidence after being arrested, the officer must then read that person their Miranda Rights prior to asking those questions. However, that does not include providing a suspect with his Miranda Rights for remedial questions or for those questions asked prior to requesting a blood, breath, or urine test.

It is something that I have been fighting for years. In my opinion, a person's Constitutional Rights, especially in a DUI case, should require that the officer advise a person of his Constitutional Rights, pursuant to Miranda, *prior* to a blood, breath, or urine test. There is actually an Arizona Supreme Court case which states that an officer should read a suspect there Miranda rights prior to a blood, breath, or urine test. However, that is considered "Dicta" (a statement of opinion that is legally relevant but isn't binding), and I have yet to find any court that has followed that Arizona Supreme Court opinion.

In short, a police officer does not have to inform a person of his Miranda Rights prior to a blood, breath, or urine test; nor is the officer required to read someone his Miranda rights at all. However, that does not mean that you are not able to exercise your Constitutional Rights. If, for some reason, you are aware of your Constitutional Rights, you can absolutely ask for an Attorney prior or subsequent to an arrest. It is still Constitutionally required that you be given access to an Attorney—although that is currently under attack as well.

Defense Attorneys are on the frontline fighting these issues, and protecting people's Constitutional Rights. Unfortunately, as we come up on the 50th anniversary of the United States Supreme Court's Miranda decision, Constitutional Rights are being chipped away, left and right. There have been attacks on the Right to Remain Silent. There have been attacks on the Right to Counsel. Pretty soon, Miranda rights and a person's Constitutional Rights will be completely meaningless. State legislatures modify laws several times a year. Sometimes citizens simply do not see the changes as they happen. This trend is unfortunate because it takes a great deal of time, money, and effort to fight Constitutional injustices.

If you get pulled over for a DUI, the safest and best way to help yourself is to tell the officer that you are invoking your Right to Remain Silent. It is also an excellent idea to tell the officer that you want to speak with a Lawyer immediately. Any diversion from these direct statements or anything that applies a condition to an unequivocal statement can later be challenged by the prosecutor as not truly being a Constitutional invocation of the Right to Remain Silent or the Right to Counsel. If someone were to say, "You know, I think it might be a good idea for me to have an Attorney present," the Courts have held that this type of statement is not an unequivocal request for an Attorney. Courts have been known to go out of their way to find that someone has not invoked their Constitutional Rights. There are numerous cases where the Court has held that the suspect was simply having an internal dialogue, spoken out loud; or was simply asking the officer as to whether he *should* invoke his Right to Remain Silent, or his Right to Counsel, but did not actually go so far as to actually invoke his Constitutional Rights. You need to be very firm and tell the officer that you are invoking your Right to Remain Silent, and that you want to contact an Attorney immediately.

The police officer is supposed to abide by a person's unequivocal invocation of his Right to Remain Silent. If, for some reason, the officer does not abide by a clear invocation, and the officer begins asking questions, the Attorney should be able to have those statements suppressed. There is a benefit in using a direct statement to invoke your Right to Remain Silent. If an unequivocal statement has been made, the officer is not allowed to testify before a jury that that statement was made, or indicate in any way that the person invoked the Right to Remain Silent. The officer also cannot tell the jury that the suspect requested an Attorney because, in doing so, the officer would be violating the person's Constitutional Rights. I once had a client facing 6 to 15 years in prison get acquitted by the Court because an officer mentioned to the jury that the Defendant invoked the Right to Remain Silent.

On the other hand, if someone wavers in his indication, and says something that is not as direct, that statement may later be used against him in court. If the person says, "Well, you know, I think maybe I should stay quiet and not answer your questions," that doesn't help. Anything that is less than an unequivocal and direct invocation of one's Right to Remain Silent, or Right to an Attorney, may end up being used against him at trial.

OTHER CONSEQUENCES OF A DUI

Any DUI conviction comes with jail time, fines and fees, license suspension or revocation, and in nearly all cases, an Ignition Interlock Device. Additional consequences can include the requirements of having SR22 High Risk Insurance, Community Restitution, and years of probation.

Other consequences of a DUI can include embarrassment, loss of job opportunities, loss of a career, and depression.

Most everyone can overcome a Misdemeanor DUI conviction. Felony Aggravated DUI convictions are much harder.

Teachers, nursing students, and nurses all have difficulty in their careers, simply for being *arrested* for DUI. Teachers can have their fingerprint clearance cards taken away, preventing them from working, simply for being arrested. Nurses can be fired, or placed on leave, due to a DUI arrest and/or a DUI conviction. And Nursing students sometimes find that the schools will not let them continue with their education while a DUI case is pending. And more recently, it appears that someone who has simply been arrested for DUI will find it very difficult, if not impossible, to go into the field of law enforcement.

People who are facing DUI charges need to make sure that they have a support group, who will help them through this difficult time. Unfortunately, some people charged with DUI go through depression, and many people turn to alcohol or drugs to ease their depression—which opens up the possibility of additional DUI cases. I once had a client with five pending DUI cases, because that client simply would not learn that lesson.

OTHER THINGS YOU SHOULD KNOW

When an officer has reasonable suspicion to stop a vehicle, he is looking for signs and symptoms of impairment related to alcohol, drugs, or medication. The officer is looking for bloodshot and watery eyes, an odor of alcohol, flushed face, slurred speech, dilated pupils, droopy eyelids, etc. In fact, the officer is looking for anything that gives the impression that the driver was consuming alcohol, using medication, or using drugs, which might impair his or her ability to drive a motor vehicle.

Since police officers are investigating what they believe to be a crime, they try to get as much information from the driver as possible, prior to placing him (or her) under arrest, and prior to reading him his Miranda Rights. One of the most damning pieces of information that the officer tries to get is an admission to consuming alcohol or using drugs. The officer might also try to get the person to rate himself on a scale of 0 to 10 for impairment. Anything that a suspect says in response to these questions will be used against him in court, and those statements can substantially hurt his case.

Everyone has a Constitutional Right to Remain Silent, and should utilize this right by refusing to answer the officer's questions. It is within your Constitutional Rights to tell an officer that you are choosing not to answer questions, or that you are "invoking your right to remain silent." If you tell the officer that you are Invoking Your Right to Remain Silent, that fact cannot be used against you in a court of law. The more a person talks, the more problems there are in the case. You should be cordial to the officer. However, that does not mean that you must be so cooperative that you give the officer all of the evidence that the officer is seeking.

A person can refuse to take a portable breath test at the scene without incurring any real consequences for refusing to take that test. If the officer asks for a blood, breath, or urine test, however, refusing that type of test does have severe consequences.

In Arizona, a refusal to submit to a blood/breath/urine test, as requested by the officer, results in at least a one-year license suspension. The officer would then very likely obtain a warrant from a judge or magistrate to draw the person's blood to be tested. Generally speaking, I do recommend that people consent to the requested blood, breath, or urine test after an arrest. If, however, the person did refuse the requested test, and the test was taken by way of a warrant, it is imperative that the person get in touch with a DUI Attorney A.S.A.P., in order to challenge, and possibly void, that one-year license suspension.

Arizona law states that a person shall be allowed access to an Attorney prior to any requested blood, breath, or urine test, so long as the request does not interfere with the investigation. The person should be given access to an Attorney upon request for an Attorney in unequivocal terms. An officer should provide access to a phone and a phone book, and allow for the suspect's privacy, if requested by the suspect. Failure to do so can lead to the dismissal of the case. It is always a good idea to request access to counsel.

Occasionally, simply requesting an Attorney may open up the possibility of that person's license being suspended for one year. Even though there is case law in Arizona stating that a request for an Attorney, standing alone, is not considered a refusal of a blood, breath, or urine test, and should not result in a one-year license suspension. It is an issue that often must be argued with the Arizona Department of Transportation.

In Arizona, there is no such thing as expungement of one's criminal record. A conviction cannot be erased. However, Arizona does allow for someone to "Set Aside" a conviction, which is something that I include as part of my representation.

If someone ends up with a DUI conviction, and after having performed all the provisions of their sentence, my clients know that they can come back to me, and I will file a Motion to Set Aside the Conviction, which will look good on their record, and in the cases of my teacher, nurse, and nursing student clients, they have all been able to resume their careers due to having their convictions "Set Aside."

Most law enforcement agencies in Arizona, unfortunately, do not use dash-cams. A few agencies do utilize on-person video cameras that officers wear on their chest, or over their ears, however, they are still quite rare. Although there are currently only a few officers in the Maricopa County area (where I practice) who have these devices, the Maricopa County Sheriff's Office is required to have them on every deputy as part of a Racial Profiling Lawsuit. Other newsworthy events throughout the country are bringing this issue to the forefront, and efforts are underway to require cameras on every officer. In the meantime, generally speaking, it is unlikely that you will encounter an officer that has any video recording capabilities.

If, by chance, the traffic stop is being recorded, that absolutely makes the case easier for everyone. It means that there is actual, physical evidence that the Attorney and client can rely upon, rather than simply trusting the officer's narrative police report. Out of the few cases that have actually had a video recording, I have seen a huge benefit for the client. Recently, one of my cases was dismissed when the officer said that the client was driving without their headlights on, which was the reason for the stop. However, since the incident happened to be captured on a dash-cam, it was clear that the client's headlights were properly illuminated, in direct opposition to the statement of the officer.

In another recent case, the officer stated that the client stumbled as he got out of the vehicle, and that he had to hold on to the side of his vehicle in order to maintain his balance. The videotape clearly showed that not only did the client not stumble when exiting the vehicle, he never even touched the side of his vehicle to maintain his balance, nor was he even swaying. The video revealed that the officer's reported observations were completely false.

The purpose of hiring an Attorney who focuses on DUI is for the Attorney to see the issues in the case that may be overlooked by the average person, an inexperienced Attorney, or a Public Defender. There are many different issues that might lead to evidence being suppressed, or a case being dismissed, but if you have the wrong person representing you, he might miss the issue in the case. You may then face a conviction that you would not have otherwise had or serve more jail or prison time than was necessary. I have taken over many cases from Public Defenders and other private Attorneys who did not see the issues that I saw, and when the client decided to fire the other Lawyer and hire me, it has lead to a much better plea agreement or the case being dismissed.

BOTTOM LINE

My best advice is that if you consume any alcohol or take any illegal drugs, stay far away from the driver's seat of a vehicle.

If you were to get pulled over for a DUI, keep in mind that you have a Constitutional Right to Remain Silent. Utilize it. You do not have to lie to the officer—I do not recommend lying to a police officer at all—but you do not have to be completely open and honest. Just politely tell the officer that you are invoking your Right to Remain Silent.

If the officer wants to do a field sobriety test to gather evidence to be used against you, do not give the officer that evidence. Refuse the field sobriety test.

You have the Constitutional Right to Consult with an Attorney. Utilize it. Tell the officer that you wish to contact an Attorney immediately. It is a good idea to make it clear that you are not refusing any sort of blood, breath, or urine test, but that you do want to consult with an Attorney in order to make an informed decision on what to do.

Most people hurt themselves because they give up everything to the police. Stop rating yourself on scales of 0 to 10 or scales of 1 to 10. Stop admitting to consuming alcohol. Stop performing the field sobriety tests. This is evidence, admissions, and confessions that hurt people.

If you do not give the officers evidence, then the prosecution will not have the evidence necessary to prove their case; which will make the case that much better for you. There is no sense in helping the prosecution to build a case against you. It is the prosecution's job to build a case against you, and you do not need to help them.

If a case has been filed against you, the best thing you can do is to have an experienced DUI Lawyer help you through this situation.

(This content should be used for informational purposes only. It does not create an attorney-client relationship with any reader and should not be construed as legal advice. If you need legal

advice, please contact an attorney in your community who can assess the specifics of your situation.)

4

MACHIAVELLI AND THE PRESUMPTION OF INNOCENCE

by Joseph Weimortz, Jr., Esq.

Joseph Weimortz, Jr., Esq.

Falangetti & Weimortz
Long Beach, California
www.westcoastdefense.com

Joseph Weimortz, Jr. became a Ventura County Deputy District Attorney in 1996 and was Deputy District Attorney for Los Angeles County for 12 years. He left the District Attorney's Office to pursue private practice in October of 2008 with his partner, Anthony Falangetti.

Attorney Weimortz, Jr. has been recognized by numerous legal publications and by his peers as one of the top criminal defense attorneys in the state of California. He was recognized as California Super Lawyers® for 2014, an honor given to less than 5% of lawyers throughout the state.

In addition, he has been chosen to the list of The National Top 100 Trial Lawyers. Membership is extended only to an exclusive group of trial lawyers who exhibit the highest legal standards of leadership, influence, stature and profile.

He regularly lectures on various topics to his peers in the legal profession, and his firm is recognized as being among the top defense law firms in Southern California.

MACHIAVELLI AND THE PRESUMPTION OF INNOCENCE

In this chapter, I want to discuss a growing problem in the legal system here in California, perhaps in every state. There is an interesting, and often devastating, desensitization among law enforcement when it comes to the subject of arresting citizens for DUI charges. First of all, understand that there is very good reason to have laws that protect against endangering others. DUI laws and their enforcement, when they are carried out judiciously, can have a positive impact upon the safety of our highways. All of that being said, when I see what's happening with DUI charges today, I am outraged. The reason for this anger is—at least in the law enforcement world—accusing someone of these charges is not taken seriously enough. Somehow, we've managed to make slapping somebody with a DUI a common thing—just another day at the office—but these charges can completely dismantle the lives of people who are, very often, innocent. Particularly in California where everyone commutes to work and effective public transportation was successfully undermined by the automobile industry decades ago.

When a cardiologist does seven or eight heart surgeries a week, she may think of it as "just a little open heart surgery," but to the person who is going under the knife, it's a very big deal. The same is true with DUI cases.

There are extreme DUIs to be sure—people who are repeat offenders who have serious drinking problems and need help— but, most of the time, the people I see in my practice are in the middle of their first and only negative experience with law enforcement. These are people who are never going to be arrested in any other context. They're the people you're drinking with at happy hour. They're secretaries, engineers, teachers, doctors, and business people. If you had a snapshot of the average DUI offender, he'd look just like you or me. So for your average DUI, the person is probably just barely at or over the legal limit, but they are scared, and they are totally humiliated.

Back in the mid to late part of the 20thcentury, the legal window for blood alcohol content (BAC) in much of the country was 0.15. Then in 1969, California adopted the United States Secretary of Transportation's standard and enacted BAC limit of 0.10[1]. This remained the BAC limit in California for many years, until the Legislature dropped it to 0.08 in 1990[2], which was before I became a District Attorney in the 1990s. Now they're talking about dropping it to a 0.05.

How is it that back then, you weren't impaired until you're 0.15, but now, magically, we're thinking about dropping it to a 0.05? Did human biology change? Have there been massive advances in the scientific study of alcohol and the human body since 1990? Are cars somehow harder to drive than in 1990? The answer to these questions is of course "no", but two things have changed: the courts and the arresting agencies are increasingly dependent on the fines generated from DUI convictions; lobbying groups have been able to sway legislators with campaign contributions and the promise of voters at the poll.

In California, big, big money is generated from DUI fines. Those fines go to the courts system, but they also go back to the agencies, like the local police department, and the prosecutor's offices. Now, because people have been brain-washed by the propaganda of lobbying groups and because they don't realize that these breath machines are really very flawed, they don't fight the charges and take the conviction and the fines that go with it. So, when an officer arrests three DUIs in one night, you have a single officer generating in excess of $5400.00 in fines, penalties and assessments for the state of California. That is a lot of money.

Now we have a citizen who will have this heinous conviction on his public record for the rest of his life. His Constitutional rights may have been trampled upon and he doesn't even know it. This is a result of the fact that the presumption of innocence doesn't really exist anymore. The fraud—the myth about what constitutes driving under the influence—has been perpetrated on the American public for years. It's essentially too much of a good thing. It's so good, in fact, that they just keep layering it on. No candidate for state legislature in California thinks "I'm going to go to the Assembly or the Senate and reduce the number of existing laws and write no new laws." They all think "If I write a new DUI law those nice ladies from that lobbying group will call me tough on crime and get me money and votes!" Unfortunately the legislature never handles something with just enough force. They are always on a pendulum that swings from one extreme to another and they rarely spend much time in the middle where good laws are made. If you tell the legislature "This dish needs a little more spice", their solution there is to dump in every bottle in the kitchen cabinet. It's overkill and it can be tragic.

I consider what I'm about to say a very conservative idea, actually. It's the idea that every day in court, whether it's a DUI or any other kind of case, we walk in and we are trying to limit the power of the government over the individual. It doesn't matter whether that particular individual is guilty or whether the charge appropriate. It's all about whether or not the rights of this individual should be defended as our Constitution requires. When you go into the courtroom, you, as a lawyer, are defending the rights of society as a whole. If you believe in small government and individual liberty, then you should recognize that it is the protection afforded by the Constitution, which makes our society possible. Occasionally we hear somebody say, "He got off on a technicality." That is pure hogswollop created by the media to outrage readers and sell advertising. Nobody ever got off on a technicality.

The technicality to which such unpatriotic fools are referring is the Constitution of the United States of America, and I refuse to call the Constitution a 'technicality.' I think it's a brilliant document that, for the first time in human history, has allowed citizens to have any kind of equality with those who govern them.

Sadly, though, there are constantly efforts to erode those rights. For example, take the cop who thinks he knows what's best for you and everyone else. Ask him, "Where do you fall on the political spectrum?" He's going to tell you that he's conservative. Nevertheless, Officer Jim represents an overreaching government. He believes, in this particular case, it is okay to fudge just a little because Jim knows in his heart the person he's pulled over is mostly guilty; so it's okay to step on the rights of this individual. It's okay to tweak the report. It's okay to check the box that says "slurred speech" because no one is ever going to know, are they?

"You know what?" He thinks to himself, "We took that man off the road tonight. Now, everybody's safer and we're the heroes. He might not have been under the influence, but just in case he was, nobody will have to deal with a mangled car full of dead nuns and orphans."

When I get up each morning to deal with the system, I am stunned to realize how well-meaning people can, whether police, prosecutors, or judges, walk into court and systematically erode the rights of individuals across the nation. I find it funny that liberals want to be perceived as tough on crime and conservatives want to be perceived as tough on crime. That leaves very few folks to walk in and fight for the Constitution. The funny thing is, those first ten amendments of the Constitution, which so many have bravely fought and bled for, all have to do with limiting the power of the government over the individual person. The 4th, 5th, 6th, and 8th Amendments in the Bill of Rights explicitly protect those accused of a crime. The 1st, 2nd, 9th and arguably 10th implicitly protect People from being accused of a crime by placing limits on what can be labeled illegal.

My law partner frequently reminds me that the 'criminal defense attorney' is the only occupation that's actually mentioned in the

Constitution. At the intersection of the Constitution and Capitalism is one of the most American of all jobs, the criminal defense attorney in private practice. Nevertheless we are maligned by the very citizenry we protect. We are seen as vultures because we are able to charge according to our skill level, instead of I don't know, working for free as though we were in a communist country. Next time you are at that grocery store don't take any form of payment. Ask the grocer if you can have your groceries Pro Bono and then let me know how dinner goes that night. If you are diagnosed with cancer you should find the best oncologist you can afford and if you are accused of a DUI or any other crime you should hire the best attorney you can afford. That is our system folks, embrace it and celebrate it, do not criticize it. I for one am glad to live in a country where hard work, sacrifice and skill is rewarded. A service of great value is rarely free.

Until most people are accused of a crime they do not realize justice is a process, not a result. When you focus on achieving a result over protecting the process you convict the innocent. I protect that process every day, and I'm glad to do it when it comes to crimes like DUI. I have to try to do my part to make sure that nobody is walking on my client's rights just to achieve a result.

Here's an interesting example of how this happens: we had one lady who was pulled over. Now, some departments have what's called MVARS, or Mobile Video Audio Recording Systems. The police officer who pulled this woman over was a CHP officer in Pasadena. He was not on the freeways, but he's still a police officer throughout the state, so he still has theoretical jurisdiction. On camera, he runs a red light taking a right-hand turn, and then he pulls the woman over two blocks away for taking a right-hand turn on the red light, which all by itself makes you just shake your head in disbelief. When the officer turns on his overhead lights, she immediately pulls over and parks. In the initial interview, she tells the officer that she's had nothing to drink. The officer claims to smell the odor of an alcoholic beverage. The field sobriety exercises are done off-camera, of course. Strangely, they always do them off-camera, and none of the evidence is preserved. He claimed that she failed to follow some of his instructions, however remember officers will tell you these "tests" are not "pass/fail".

When you watch the part of the encounter that was filmed, her sobriety is obvious. When she was questioned she knew exactly where she was and where she was going and what time it was. Her speech was not slurred. She had red, watery eyes and that is supposed to be an objective symptom of alcohol consumption, but red, watery eyes can also be caused by any number of other things. If you have red, watery eyes, it might be an objective symptom of the fact that it's one in the morning.

She is so steady on her feet that in the video we subpoenaed from the jail, as they're walking her into the jail, she's actually wearing four-inch heels with her hands cuffed behind her back. The officers are so confident in her ability to balance and safely walk that they didn't even bother holding her by the elbow as she walked up a ramp. Nevertheless, they will testify that they had probable cause to believe she was under the influence. So, she now has to hire an attorney to defend her in a DUI case under those circumstances.

This woman did hire an attorney—us. If she hadn't been sure of her innocence and willing to fight for her rights, if she hadn't found the right attorneys, she might have ended up with her first DUI.

COMMON MISTAKES

I hope that when you've finished this chapter, you will understand a little better about where and how your rights are being trampled upon. You can stand up for yourself by hiring an attorney, but until you get un-brainwashed, you're just another target on the highway. To follow, I've listed some common mistakes people make when they've been arrested for DUI.

DON'T CALL A LAWYER

When you've been arrested, and you imagine, for whatever reason, that you're guilty, you may not be inclined to call a lawyer. You might just tell yourself to pay the piper. "Do you need a lawyer for a DUI?" You absolutely do, if for no other reason than to un-brainwash you. Let a defense lawyer sit down with you and explain to you how the system works, what the possible defenses are, and what might have been done wrong in your case. Before you decide to just "take your punishment," be your own advocate for a moment. People generally have a fairly good foundation when it comes to right and wrong, but they will make erroneous conclusions based upon bad information, such as two drinks equal .08, and they will become their own judge and jury. Guilty as charged.

Please be a little kinder to yourself. Allow the system to work as it's supposed to.

CHATTING WITH THE OFFICER

The officer will ask, "How much did you have to drink?" The guy behind the wheel will say, "Two drinks," regardless of how much he really had because the little alcohol chart the DMV sends you says that two drinks of un-metabolized alcohol in your blood stream is just under a 0.08.

Then the officer asks, "When did you stop drinking?" The driver, being the bright human that he is, thinks, "Well, if I can put this as far away in time from my driving, maybe I can work some psychology on the officer." (As if you were the first person to hatch such a plan.) So, he says, "I stopped drinking three hours ago."

The truth is, his buddies urged him to have one more drink for the road, and he did.

By placing his last drink three hours previous to being stopped, he has probably thrown away his best defense. The irony is that it will take some time for the alcohol he's consumed to be absorbed into his system.

Here's an analogy. Stand at the bathroom sink and turn both taps on full blast with the drain open. The water flowing from the nozzle is your drinking pattern and how much you drink. The drain is your liver, which is metabolizing the alcohol. The water rising in the sink is your blood alcohol. In the case of alcohol the water is not poured into the sink immediately depending on a number of factors, such how much you have had to eat.

You have a shot. You get in your car. That shot hasn't been absorbed yet. When you get pulled over for something like expired tags, they're still going to do a DUI investigation on you. Here's a bit of inside information: People need to know that whatever reason they are given for being pulled over at night, the real reason the cop pulled you over is he wants to see if you are DUI. They walk up to your car. The first thing they're looking for is the smell of alcohol coming out of that car.

The reality is that the alcohol hasn't absorbed in your system because you just drank it 15 minutes before you got into the car. At the time you're driving, you're probably not above 0.08, but then, by the time they take you back to the station 30 minutes later and it's had a chance to absorb now you are over an 0.08. (They don't give you this information on the little chart from the DMV.) Your overactive conscience kicks in, you find yourself guilty in the court of "I've been very bad," and now you're going for a ride in the police cruiser. The young cop who's writing bad reports or making mistakes in his investigation won't have to go to court and be challenged, so he just keeps doing it. Then poor investigations become part of a culture for his station as he passes on flawed investigation shortcuts to the next new cop.

TRUSTING THE TESTS

Since you've probably never had this experience, allow me to tell you what the police are looking for when they stop you. First thing they're looking for is a driving pattern. Know that anything can be a driving pattern. They just want a legal excuse to pull you over, especially if it's after 1:30 a.m. Once they pull you over, they stroll up to the side of your car. The next thing they're looking for is how you interact with them and whether or not there's a smell of alcohol coming from the car. They check to see if you have red, watery eyes. Is your speech slurred when you speak with them? If they ask you to get out of the car, they watch to see if you have an unsteady gait as you walk to wherever they direct you.

In California, the form police use has four boxes defining the objective symptoms of intoxication. It's a lot easier to just check a box than to make busy law enforcement officers write it all out. Unfortunately, it's also psychologically easier for that officer to just check a box than to affirmatively write out an observation that is a falsehood or an exaggeration. Think about it. How easy it is to say, "Who will ever know?" and just check a box. I have a lot of respect for law enforcement. I'm not implying that they all lie or that those who lie, lie all the time. I am saying that a certain percentage of them lie, exaggerate or omit information helpful to the client because they don't think it's a big deal. Does that feel like a lie if you make a check mark? If they actually wrote it out, even that little tiny difference would make things better.

So, they have their four symptoms and then they start asking the pre-investigatory questions, which the Supreme Court case, *Berkemer v. McCarty*, (1984) 468 U.S. 420, gives the officer the right to ask before he reads you your Miranda rights.

Cleverly, this is when they start trying to eliminate defenses. They may lead you to say things that can later be used by the prosecutor to trip you up and imply that you tell lies. That hurts a lot of people. Typical questions are: Where were you drinking tonight? What were you drinking? When did you start drinking? When did you stop? Then they'll ask you a question like, "What did you have to eat," because when you ate can affect the absorption rate and that goes to the rising blood alcohol defense. It's the best defense that there is in my personal opinion, because it resonates with human experience. From Sinatra's "One more for my Baby and One for the Road" to Dave Matthews "Grace is Gone", the idea of one last drink before leaving the bar is cultural. Ironically, science tells us that if you are driving a short distance, that drink is not the problem because it is not absorbed. It will however show up in your blood stream by the time you are arrested and taken to the station for a blood or breath test.

At this point, they start looking for specific, unusual defenses by asking questions like: Are you epileptic? Are you diabetic? (If you're diabetic, you could have a diabetic reaction that may affect the breath test.) Are you under the care of a doctor or a dentist? Are you taking any medicine? Is there anything wrong with your car? (These questions are formulated to eliminate alternative reasons for your driving pattern.)

They get to ask you all those questions before they've read you your rights, and then they get to ask you to get out of the car. Officers who are better trained start running through the National Highway and Traffic Safety tests. They look for Horizontal Gaze Nystagmus—whether or not your eyes jump around when you're trying to follow the motion of an object like a pen—even though those symptoms occur with a certain part of the population naturally and especially in people who have had head injuries. This part of the test is not being filmed, mind you. Here you have a cop with a light and a pen. He's holding it away from your face looking for the angle at which your eyes start to bounce, and he's doing this on the side of the road at night with nothing memorializing that evidence.

Then they do the Romberg's test, which I love. In order to test your ability to balance, they ask you to stand with your feet together, head tilted back and eyes closed. You are told to estimate 30 seconds. You estimate it at 30 seconds, but really it was 25 seconds. Some cops don't know that it's a plus or minus 10-second test—perhaps they forget that as they get older. In any case, they mark you down for that, which your lawyer must correct later. At that point on the report, he mentions that you swayed in all directions. (Swaying is natural and normal here, but it's only acceptable if you sway two inches or less in any direction.)

So, now you do the "walk and turn" test. Nine steps forward, nine steps back, heel to toe. They'll write down if there's a gap between your feet even though the National Highway Traffic Safety Administration says there can be a one-inch gap. They make notes about whether or not you sway. (Remember, while standing, that sway has to be over two inches anyway.) Then they'll do the "One-Leg Stand" test. After all of this, these officers are supposed to bring their expertise to bear and come to a conclusion about your sobriety. (Don't let this worry you. We know that, statistically, the officer made up his mind about arresting you back at the Horizontal Gaze test.)

Mind you, if you don't do any of those things and you refuse to take their tests, they will make a decision regarding your level of intoxication regardless of your refusal to cooperate. You're still going to jail. They're not really putting any weight on any of this testing, anyway.

For my part, I would not take field sobriety exercises for any reason. I weigh over 300 pounds and I'm 6' 5". I was an athlete, so I have had injuries to my ankles and knees. The idea that my goals in life are going to hinge upon my ability to perform these physical tests, like walking on a line, gives me heartburn. I just don't think you can legitimately compare the way a 6' 5" man with long legs walks a line with the way a 5' 1" woman who weighs 100 pounds walks on the same line. This is why they don't film this stuff, because it's entirely subjective.

COURT OR JURY TRIAL?

Now, you've been charged. Do you want to appear just before a judge in a court trial, or do you want a jury of your peers? The answer is easy. You should never, ever do a court trial. It's my personal belief that jurors make their decision with their hearts and rationalize with their minds. A judge, on the other hand, is going to be more cynical about the defense evidence. You have a better chance of getting a not guilty verdict when you have 12 people deciding your fate versus one judge. So, you really should never do a court trial for any reason.

If you go into court for a DUI and you hang the jury at 10-2, the judge might not give the prosecution permission for that case to be retried, or he might put you in a position to negotiate it down to something less. The lawyer makes more money when he conducts a court trial because the lawyer doesn't have to spend two days selecting a jury and then another three to four days trying the case. They can just leap in and do a shorter version of the case. In my personal opinion, I don't think that can ever be good for the client.

People don't understand how fallible the BAC testing can be. There are a lot of flaws with the machines and how the tests are administered and the lawyer's job is to educate the jury. When they do see film of the defendant, or listen to audio of the arrest, they anticipate that the person is going to be obviously under the influence. When one of those cases is being tried in which the accused does not appear under the influence at all, there is more room for argument. Having a jury that is open-minded and that will listen to the evidence and make the other side prove their case is beneficial to the defendant. As for me, I like people on DUI juries that are engineers because I think that the uncertainty of the machines is something that concerns them.

A WORD ABOUT MOUTH ALCOHOL

I don't want to put you to sleep with a lot of very technical stuff, but you need to know about mouth alcohol. Ideally, breath test machines are meant to check for evidence of alcohol that has already been metabolized by your body and is now being emitted in your breath through the lungs. Some breath-testing machines are equipped with what's called a "slope detector." This "slope detector" repeatedly samples breath to identify any alcohol that may linger in the mouth or is the product of fumes coming up from the stomach. If you have a faulty valve in your stomach, or suffer from Gastro Esophageal Reflux Disease, GERD, the alcohol you just swallowed—which has not yet made it to your bloodstream—can be measured along with the legitimate lung-based sample, which will give you a false reading on a machine without a slope detector.

I had always wondered how real mouth alcohol was as a defense, particularly in relation to the PAS (Preliminary Alcohol Screening). The PAS test is the handheld breath test they offer you in the field to get a reading of your BAC closer in time to driving and combat the "rising blood alcohol" defense. That particular machine they use in the field is usually not equipped with a "slope detector."

One evening, I was at the house of a fellow DUI lawyer. It happens that this guy owns an Alco-Sensor IV, the exact same model that's used by the police, so I decided to test the thing. I blew into it before I'd had anything to drink. My BAC was at 0.00, which is where it should have been. Then I took one mouthful of Corona, swallowed it, waited a beat, and then blew into it again, and I was a 0.06. As I said, I'm 6'5", about 300 pounds. At my weight, I estimate that to get to a 0.06 legitimately, I probably would have needed to consume three to four drinks in an hour. Just one blow, close in time to having taking a swig, and I was very close to a legally drunk reading on the machine, which was impossible. Because of my excess weight, I'm more subject to acid reflux disease, so that was probably part of that high reading. Nevertheless, unless there is a "slope detector," the reading is going to be high and false.

Before you even start to explore that idea, there are flaws with the actual algorithm itself which converts breath alcohol to a blood alcohol reading, meaning that it doesn't work on the whole population. There is no certainty that a 0.08 on a breath test equals a 0.08 on a blood test on every individual. The algorithm is so flawed the legislature has written the law so that it prevents defense attorneys from arguing it on the over 0.08 count. In California, if you have a 0.08 or above on the breath machine then you're in violation of the law. Period.

CALIFORNIA'S GIANT CASH COW

One of the other benefits I have, because I used to be a District Attorney, is that I've ridden along with California Highway Patrol officers on nights when they are specifically looking for DUIs.

They'll pull people over for speeding, but once they realize that there's not a DUI investigation with this individual, they will often let the subject go because they don't want to be slowed down. In a sense, these officers are in competition with other officers to see which team can get the most DUIs. It's an unofficial competition, but it's a natural one. Everybody who is in any kind of job competes with their friends on some level. It's what keeps things from getting boring. So, if they go out on patrol during the night shift, which is specifically looking for DUIs, and one team hooks up three DUIs that night while the other team hooks up zero, well then, Team A has bragging rights and they'll give each other a hard time.

All of that contributes to the culture where the officers themselves are desensitized to the person they are arresting and the possible consequences it will have on their lives. It's something of a game now. So, that's why there have been examples in California of officers who've been caught submitting the same basic report over and over again. I look at it from the iceberg perspective; 90 percent of the iceberg is underwater. Most of what's happening in our police departments is invisible because it happens under our radar. We may see 10 percent of the problem, but there's so much more you cannot see. The roach analogy also works. If you find a roach in your house and you kill it, your house is not roach-less. He's got a family.

If a defense attorney catches one police officer submitting multiple reports where they don't even bother to change the symptomology or the basic facts, he should not assume that he's solved the bigger problem; other officers are doing this as well. I honestly think it happens not because police are consciously evil, but because they are afraid that if you're close, it's better to take you off of the highway. Their job is to save lives and they fear, "If you're close, maybe you're not actually guilty, but it's better go ahead and arrest you." That officer imagines that the worst thing that's going to happen to you is you're going to stay in jail for a few hours, come out, and have to plead guilty and experience a license restriction. They also have the experience that this is something that can happen to anybody—they know this because they do it every day. They don't take it seriously when they jam somebody with a DUI, because they don't think anything really ugly is going to happen in the person's life. That's so wrong.

Many cops realize just how serious a DUI conviction is only when they see another police officer get one. Then, in a heartbeat, it's, "Whoa! Wait a second. I drive for a living. If I can't drive for 30 days or for a year on a refusal, that means that I can't do my job. If I can't do my job, that means that I can be fired. If I can be fired, that means I might lose my pension." It's a domino effect of consequences that happens every day in the lives of the individuals on the street. The police officers are generally desensitized to the life-altering consequences of treating DUI charges like a game.

The consequences are huge. The DUI has become a cash cow for the state. Here's what we do here in California. (I'm going to try not to rant, I swear!) I was on the other side for a long time. I have a lot of respect for prosecutors and I enjoyed being a prosecutor, but I will tell you that doing both sides is a very eye-opening experience. There is a maximum fine of $1,000 set by the legislature, but rather than going up to the legislature to raise the fine, the counties decided that they could play a little word game and add penalties and assessments to those statutory fines. As a result, a $400 fine now ends up costing you about $2,000.

The penalty and the assessments multiply the base fine. They just call them P and A's. They don't even bother to split them apart. Then, they throw on a couple of other costs, like a court security fee or your county crime lab fee, depending on where you are. At the end of the day, it's the penalties and assessments and the county's ability to assess them without going to the legislature that becomes a staggering multiplier on the fine. Seriously, if you get a fine for $1,000, you can expect to pay about $4,000. That's the way it works in California, and I believe they are quite proud of it. I think the state considers itself to be a leader in the prosecution of driving under the influence.

I'm not saying that a DUI is not serious, but I am saying it's being overblown (no pun intended). I used to prosecute murders. I can tell you that the primary causes of criminal deaths in California are gangs and domestic violence, but if you listen to the politicians and Mothers Against Drunk Driving, you would think that the primary source of death is DUI-related homicides. My partner was in a murder-specific unit. I was not. Nevertheless, in my career with LA County, I can tell you that I handled probably about 20 murder cases. Out of those, I would say that perhaps two of them were the result of somebody being involved with a driver under the influence. I see the DUI problem as something of a mythical giant. It's not nearly as big as some folks would have you believe.

If you're a new legislator, all you need to do is write a new law making it harder on either sex offenders or DUI drivers. When you bring such a law, you're starting to build your legacy. Who's going to say "no" to a law that's hard on perverts and drunks? So, it just becomes this kind of ever-growing coral reef of additional penalties and restrictions. What's ironic and very unfortunate about California, particularly in the southern part of the state, is that you're in an area that, back in the '40s and '50s, set out deliberately to kill public transportation. Geographically, the area is very spread out, and everybody drives because there is little public transportation and most people would not be caught dead on it. If Joe Citizen is going out to have a few drinks with friends, Joe is going to drive (although Uber X and similar services are an excellent cost effective alternative). Here, few of us have the option of walking down to the local pub for a social evening with friends.

The whole thing tends to make me a little cynical. It just seems more and more like an increasingly bloated industry ran by the state. Now, obviously, I'm a private attorney and I profit from the industry too but there's something extremely distasteful to me about the state profiting from convicting people of a crime, and in fact relying upon the revenue from those convictions. To those of you who would ask me, "Yes, but what would you say to a family who lost a loved one to a drunk driver and who has advocated stricter laws?" I would remind you I'm not saying driving under the influence should be legal. To answer the question however I would say: "I'm sorry for your loss, but your loss will not be mitigated or justified by compromising our system of justice and basic freedoms to catch a few more guilty people and ruin the lives of a lot more innocent people." A lot more good people have died defending our Constitution than have lost their lives at the hands of drunk drivers. Those rights were paid for in the most precious currency there is, let's not allow them to be abridged because someone can't accept a tragedy in their own lives.

The state isn't interested in eliminating driving under the influence anyway. If the state was then why not make it zero tolerance? Why not make 0.0 the legal limit? Why not put an

Ignition Interlock Device in every car? At the risk of sounding cynical again, the reason is because in the state of California, local governments make a lot of money off of liquor licenses and the taxes on restaurants and bars. Remember, before Prohibition there was no Federal income tax. The revenue came from the production, sales and consumption of alcohol. That lesson has not been lost on the state. You don't want to kill the golden goose. You just want to find a way to get it to lay more eggs. They've managed to do that very effectively, I think. The states and counties get the goods, meaning the money and a reputation for being tough on drunks, but the price that's being paid by the innocent citizens who are funding the whole operation is just too much. They pay financially, and what's probably worse, they spend the rest of their lives being ashamed of having been arrested.

Back when I was still a prosecutor, I met a guy who was a waiter in a restaurant. He told me that he just had his second DUI. He was a stockbroker by trade until he got a second DUI. Now, he's a waiter in a restaurant because he couldn't drive for a year and the restaurant was close to where he lived. Does that punishment fit his crime? Obviously, there is a legitimate problem out there at some level with people drinking and driving, but how far on the prophylactic side are we going to go, when the evidence doesn't necessarily support that the person is a danger? Are you really too intoxicated to drive at 0.05 or was 0.08, or 0.10 or 0.15 the correct BAC? Have our human metabolisms changed that much in the last 40 years?

I urge you to realize that simply being pulled over and arrested for DUI doesn't have to be a life-changer. Understand that the tests and the people who administer them are fallible, so before you convict yourself of this crime, talk to an attorney.

(This content should be used for informational purposes only. It does not create an attorney-client relationship with any reader and should not be construed as legal advice. If you need legal advice, please contact an attorney in your community who can assess the specifics of your situation.)

———————————————

References:

[1]"The Detection of DWI at BACs Below 0.10" *U.S. Department of Transport ation National Highway Traffic Safety Administration*, Jack Stuster, PhD, CPE, Project Director, 12 Sep. 1997, http://www.drugdetection.net/NHTSA docs/Stuster Detection of DWI at BAC's below 0.10%25.pdf

[1]"The Development Of California Drunk Driving Legislation", *Bureau of Criminal Statistics and Special Services State of California*, Michael Laurence, 1988, https://www.ncjrs.gov/pdffiles1/Digitization/115797NCJRS. pdf.

[2]"A Preliminary Assessment Of The Impact Of Lowering The Illegal BAC Per Se Limit To 0.08 in Five States", *National Highway Traffic Safety Administration National Center for Statistics and Analysis Mathematical Analysis Division,* (Dec. 1994), http://www-nrd.nhtsa.dot.gov/Pubs/BAC08R PT.PDF

5

WHEN YOU REPRESENT YOURSELF, YOU HAVE A FOOL FOR A CLIENT – DON'T DO IT!

by David R. Sachs, Esq.

David R. Sachs, Esq.

Riebling, Proto & Sachs, LLP
White Plains, New York
www.rpslawyers.com

David Sachs is a partner in the law firm of Riebling, Proto and Sachs, whose exceptional legal abilities have earned him praise and accolades from his clients and throughout the legal community. He has represented countless individuals with compassion, understanding and zealous advocacy.

He began his legal career as an Assistant District Attorney with the Westchester County District Attorney's office where he prosecuted countless criminal cases and gained significant trial experience. As a prosecutor David also handled many criminal appeals which were published. After leaving the District Attorney's Office David took his vast experience into private practice.

David is admitted to practice law in all of the courts in the State of New York and in the United States Supreme Court. David regularly practices in the criminal courts, and Supreme courts of Westchester County, Bronx County, Putnam County, Dutchess County, Rockland County and Queens County.

WHEN YOU REPRESENT YOURSELF, YOU HAVE A FOOL FOR A CLIENT – DON'T DO IT!

I have been practicing in the area of criminal and DWI law for many years and I have been on both sides of the courtroom, first as a prosecutor and now as a DWI and criminal defense lawyer. Throughout the years, it has never ceased to amaze me how many people perilously believe that they can "go it alone" in the courtroom when they are arrested and charged with DWI.

These people often imagine that the truth will set them free and there is no need to have legal representation. However, this belief typically comes to an abrupt and grinding halt once that person walks into a courtroom without an attorney by his side and experiences the immediate impact that his DWI arrest has upon his ability to drive and earn a living. This happens immediately despite the fact that one is presumed innocent until proven guilty.

Working within the criminal justice system is a high-stakes situation where the weight of the government's unlimited resources will be hurled at you in an unrelenting manner. To make matters worse, the DWI laws in every state are often very complex and confusing to ordinary people. In addition, a DWI criminal conviction can and will follow you for the rest of your life in most states, which can potentially have devastating consequences. Representing yourself can cost you a lot of money—not only in the short term but also in the long term due to fines, penalties, higher insurance costs, and inhibiting your ability to actually land a decent job.

The bottom line is that the best time to learn how to be a lawyer is not when you are arrested and charged with DWI. No, the best time to do that is probably by going to law school before you are arrested for DWI. While I say this with obvious sarcasm, my point is that when you are arrested and charged with DWI, you need someone by your side immediately who has already gone to law school and is skilled and knowledgeable about DWI laws and knows how to provide you with the best possible defense. That, of course, is a DWI lawyer.

COMPLEX LAWS AND SELF-REPRESENTATION TRAPS

When people call and visit my office they are frequently reluctant to spend money on an attorney; the public often views lawyers as a bunch of money-hungry vultures who are in the business of making money. While there are bad seeds in any profession due to basic human avarice and greed, I truly believe that most DWI lawyers are, by and large, good seeds. We can have a profound and meaningful impact on your life in a DWI case. We can help you understand the complex DWI laws, guide you through them, provide you with a skilled and articulate analysis of the strengths and weaknesses of the case against you, and most importantly, we will develop the most effective defense strategy tailored specifically to the facts of your case. Then, and only then, will you have the ability to make intelligent choices throughout your DWI case.

Even if you are still unconvinced that you need a DWI lawyer, most judges in courtrooms throughout the country are extremely reluctant to allow anyone to represent oneself in a DWI case. Since a DWI charge can carry a criminal conviction, it can mean a potential loss of your civil liberties, such as jail or probation. It can also result in the loss of professional licenses. So, in spite of your wishes, the judge may require you to have a competent attorney present to represent your interests. Typically, if you cannot retain a lawyer because of your financial situation, the court will appoint an attorney to your case because judges understand that DWI laws are complex. They recognize that without a competent attorney, the law may not work for you in the way that it should.

FIELD SOBRIETY TESTING AND REFUSING THE BREATHALYZER TEST

Typically, when the police pull over a driver and conduct a DWI investigation the police will utilize what are referred to as "Field Sobriety Tests" to assist them in determining whether they have probable cause to arrest the driver for DWI. Examples of these tests include walking heel-to-toe on a straight line that is real or imaginary, balancing on one foot and touching your nose with your finger with your eyes closed. When the police officer says that the person failed one or more of the tests, many people simply think, "Well, the police officer gave me some field sobriety tests. I failed them, so there's not much I can do. How would I be able to challenge the results? It's my word against theirs." That's not true at all; field sobriety testing is far from being a black-and-white issue.

Over recent years, the National Highway Traffic Safety Administration has attempted to create a national standard for field sobriety tests by sponsoring training for police officers across the country. In fact, they've authored a training manual for the training, called *DWI Detection and Standard Field Sobriety Testing*. Many police departments across the country utilize the manual and the National Highway Traffic Safety Administration's training for more consistency.

In nearly all instances, police officers must administer the field sobriety tests in the manner set forth in the manual. In fact, the validity of the test itself depends entirely upon its proper administration by the police officer. For example, prior to administering the test, the police officer must demonstrate the test to the driver. He must also ask if the instructions are understood prior to the driver performing the tests. Many times, because police officers are also human, they simply forget to follow proper procedures and protocols. When that happens, field sobriety tests can be invalidated.

Even when the tests are administered 100 percent perfectly by police officers, the tests themselves are still not 100 percent conclusive. In fact, the manual itself states that none of the tests is more than 80 percent accurate. This means, of course, that they are 20 percent inaccurate; because people have varying intelligences, physical abilities, and abilities to follow instructions.

Human beings also have different balancing abilities. I always remind my clients that they don't have to do One-Leg Stands and Walk-and-Turn Tests and other balancing acts to get a driver's license. However, when they are being investigated for DWI, somehow their ability to operate a vehicle is totally dependent on an ability to balance in these quirky balancing tests. Even in a completely sober situation, you may be fine to drive a car, but your balancing ability may be terrible for any number of reasons.

A thorough legal and factual analysis of the administration of the field sobriety tests by an experienced and aggressive DWI attorney is vital to your defense in court. This is especially true when a DWI conviction may depend upon these tests. By having an intimate understanding of the testing protocols in the manual, an experienced lawyer can find the flaws and create a powerful defense.

In addition to not understanding field sobriety testing, many drivers do not understand the ramifications of refusing to take a breathalyzer test. While every driver has the constitutional right to refuse taking the breathalyzer test, the test refusal is often governed by state laws and evidentiary rules, which say that the refusal can be used against you to show your "consciousness of guilt" or evidence of your awareness of your responsibility for the crime.

In addition, refusing to take a breathalyzer test can have an immediate impact on your driver's license. Driver's licenses are a privilege and not a right. Because it is considered a privilege, in most states, when a driver receives a license he or she is also consenting to submitting to a breathalyzer test if suspected of driving while intoxicated. As a result, if you don't submit to the test, many states will require that your license be revoked or suspended for a designated period time. This can even happen even if you are found not guilty of DWI or even if the DWI case is dismissed for other reasons.

For example, in New York, even if you refuse a breathalyzer test and go to trial and win your case, New York State can still revoke your driving privileges for one year. As soon as you refuse a breathalyzer, that triggers an administrative hearing by the Department of Motor Vehicles (DMV) itself; it is a civil hearing totally independent of a criminal case. During that hearing, it is the burden of the police officer to demonstrate to a DMV administrative judge that there was probable cause to arrest you and that you refused the breathalyzer.

If the DMV administrative judge finds that there was probable cause to arrest you for DWI and that you refused the breathalyzer unequivocally, the DMV then revokes your license for a year. This happens regardless of the outcome of your criminal case. As is plain to see, New York requires a harsh penalty for refusing a breathalyzer test. This is why understanding the laws of your state regarding refusals of breathalyzer tests is crucial.

YOUR CONSTITUTIONAL RIGHTS

It's not unusual for me to hear this question: "How do you defend people who have committed these crimes?" (This not only means DWIs, but also many other types of cases such as murder cases, attempted murder cases, drug cases, etc.) "How can you represent these dirt bags? Why do you do it?"

Simply put, I do it because these dirt bags have the same rights as the rest of us. They are presumed innocent until proven guilty beyond a reasonable doubt by the prosecutor. This is the very cornerstone of the entire criminal justice system that has been in place since our country was founded. As lawyers, we must protect the individual rights guaranteed by our state and federal constitutions whether or not I like my client. In fact, this is part of the oath that I took when I became an attorney: to protect and defend the Constitution of the United States of America. Now, I have represented some very unsavory people, as well as some very good, very honorable people. However, my decision to represent some unsavory characters is never based on whether I like my client. If we all lived in that kind of system, many people might find it very difficult to hire an attorney. Having said all of this, despite popular belief, we attorneys DO have consciences just like everybody else! And this is part of what makes my job very challenging! But in the end, I have to set aside my personal beliefs because I took an oath. Every person who comes into my office who has been charged with a crime is an individual who deserves to have his or her rights protected. Not because I said so but because our state and federal constitutions say so.

MY REASON FOR BECOMING A DEFENSE ATTORNEY

When I was in eighth grade, I took a test at school that was supposed to reveal what type of work I should focus on when I grew up—it said, "Attorney." It matched what I already thought, that I wanted to be an attorney like my dad. I was thoroughly brainwashed. At a young age, I was always impressed with what my dad did, when he took me with him to court and to the office. My dad also taught me the function of a criminal defense attorney and he would share case stories with me and I was drawn to the idea of performing a vital function in our society.

Lawyers serve a fundamental role in our society: from drafting laws in state legislatures to protecting individuals' civil liberties, our constitutional rights. One of my very first jobs, right out of law school, was as a prosecutor. I prosecuted countless criminal cases and DWIs. My upbringing gave me a better perspective on the need for aggressive prosecution. When I went into private practice, I found that I could naturally defend the laws. In both jobs, I was protecting the laws.

YOU MAY -AND PROBABLY SHOULD - REMAIN SILENT

Our state and federal constitutions guarantee that you don't have to testify against yourself and that everything you say can and will be used against you in court. In fact, most people seem to know this concept from watching TV shows: if the police want to ask you questions, shut your mouth. Yet somehow, when people are pulled over for a DWI, they don't do that. Most people, no matter how much or little that they've had to drink, think they can talk themselves out of the situation and avoid arrest. In doing so, they typically tell the police officer that they have only had two or three drinks in an attempt to minimize the truth. The bottom line is that they shouldn't say anything. When I tell this to family or friends when they ask advice, they get all wide-eyed and ask, "So, Dave, what you're doing is advising people to try to beat a DWI arrest? Aren't you concerned that these drunk drivers are on the streets? Shouldn't you encourage them to be honest and truthful with the police officers?"

My response is that this issue has nothing to do with my conscience. Truth be told, my conscience says that I'm all in favor of tough DWI laws. This is me on the street, this is you on the street; our families are driving on the street. These drunk drivers pose a direct threat to our lives and safety every day and to everyone we know! Yes, I have a conscience. But again, this is not about my conscience. It is about our rights as citizens and being aware of our rights. As an attorney, part of my function is to inform people about their rights and how to assert their rights, not to tell them how to beat a test. That's an important distinction.

On a daily basis, innocent people who are not driving drunk, as well as those who are guilty, are stopped and asked DWI questions. One of our rights is to remain silent if we're asked questions—whether we're innocent or guilty. So here is my general advice to people, including drivers: remain silent, regardless of your guilt or innocence.

I always advise people to say nothing because there's no advantage in saying something. If you say, "I haven't had anything to drink," or (more typically) you'll say, "I had two drinks," even if you really had five, you've just told a big fat lie to a police officer in the middle of an official investigation. That big lie is going to be used as testimony against you at your trial. This is the bottom line: there's no advantage in saying anything to the police officers who are trying to conduct a DWI investigation. There is only one reason for the police officer to ask a driver a question about the drinks he or she has had: the officer is collecting information to develop probable cause to arrest you for DWI. At that particular point, there is no advantage for the driver to make any statements to the police officer.

Hard as it is, you need to just sit there, keep quiet and be polite to the police officer! You also need to remember that he is just doing his job which is a vital and important job in our society. A police officer's job is to protect us all. By pulling you over because he or she thinks you may be driving while intoxicated, whether you like it or not, that police officer is taking action to protect us; including you, the driver. Of course, when you assert your right to refuse to answer questions you always want to be polite to the police officer. There's a polite way to say, "I'm not answering that question," and there's an impolite way of saying, "I'm not going to answer that question."

So let's play this out a little bit. In a routine traffic stop— perhaps you're pulled over for a broken tail light or erratic driving—the police officer approaches the car. First, he asks for your driver's license, registration, and insurance card. This marks the actual beginning for any DWI investigation. Police officers are trained to watch for signs of alcohol intoxication. Right from the beginning, the officer begins to watch for signs of intoxication. Did you fumble for your license? Are your eyes red? Do you have slurred speech? Do you smell of alcohol, etc.? When you hand over your driver's license and registration, the officer might start asking you questions like, "Where are you coming from?" or, "Where are you going to?" It should be obvious that the best reply is not, "It's none of your business. I don't have to answer that question." Rather, in a calm voice, without a nasty attitude, you can appropriately say something like this: "Officer, I respectfully decline to answer your question."

Now, this may irritate the police officer, but that's the police officer's prerogative. There will be further investigation; once you decline to answer, that does raise the antennae of the police officer. He has already watched to see if you fumbled for your driver's license etc. Now that you won't answer his question, he may try to follow up with additional questions such as, "Have you been drinking tonight?" If you respectfully decline to answer those questions, and if he doesn't see any other indicators of intoxication (such as breath smelling like alcohol, bloodshot eyes, normal demeanor), the police officer will probably just write you a ticket for the broken tail light. However, if he sees that you're slurring your speech, smell like alcohol, looking at him with bloodshot eyes, fumbling for your license, and refusing to answer questions, he's going to say, "Get out of the car."

It's easy to see the difference. Simply declining to answer the questions will not be the deciding factor in the officer's decision to arrest you for DWI. The difference is whether or not the police officer believes that he has probable cause to arrest you based upon his entire DWI investigation.

IMMEDIATE CONSEQUENCES

Very often, at their first DWI appearance, people are shocked to learn that their license will be suspended while their case is pending even though they are presumed innocent until proven guilty. After going to court alone without an attorney, the consequences of that pronouncement can take the wind right out of their sails.

For example, a first-time offender often shows up in court alone thinking, "No big deal. I'm not really guilty. I'll tell the court that I don't feel like I'm guilty, and we'll take it from there." Then, when he shows up before the judge and pleads not guilty, he discovers that his license is being suspended. In New York, for example, at the driver's first court appearance if his arrest for DWI was also based upon a breathalyzer result or a breathalyzer test refusal, his driving privileges are suspended by the Court for 30 days on the spot. That's it, zero driving privileges for thirty days. The driver gets a shock: "I didn't know that was going to happen!" The case gets adjourned, and now this driver doesn't have a license for 30 days. What happens next? The driver gets fired from his job because he can't drive to work. Now there's no income. How will he pay bills and support himself? As immediate consequences go, this is a huge one.

If he had consulted with a DWI attorney before going to court, he would have understood that sequence. For example, in New York, he would have known that even though that suspension would happen, his attorney could request a "hardship hearing" and protect his ability to drive to and from work for the first 30 days after that first court appearance. An attorney would have gathered the proof and evidence needed to provide to the court in order to get that hardship license, so the client wouldn't get fired.

Another possible shock happens after the officer doesn't charge the defendant with every applicable crime, either because he missed the clues or because the officer was being generous. The prosecutor can later add on more charges to the original charge(s). For example, one of my clients was charged with a DWI plus a traffic ticket, for failure to signal a right turn. After the case was submitted to the prosecutor, a flurry of eight additional tickets was added before our first court appearance. This same scenario could happen with additional criminal charges. It's the prerogative of the prosecutor to add on charges if he or she feels that it's appropriate to do so.

These are the kinds of things that drivers need to know to protect their livelihoods. They are the also the kinds of things they learn from an experienced DWI attorney. Here is an illustration of what can happen if the driver doesn't have a DWI attorney by their side at all times throughout their DWI case. One of my clients came into my office after already pleading guilty to criminal DWI. When he pled guilty, in addition to being sentenced to three years of probation, he received a six month revocation of his driver's license. When he reported to probation, the probation officer told him, "You get to re-apply for your driver's license when we say so, and not before then. You're on probation for three years, so we have control over your right to re-apply for your driver's license during that entire three year period." When he heard this, the client was in shock. It turns out that the probation officer was correct. It also turned out that the reason that the client was not aware of this fact was that he was represented by a "family friend" who was a real estate lawyer.

Any experienced DWI attorney would have explained this to the client before he pled guilty and received three years of probation. As it turns out, if the client had known this, he would not have pled guilty and would have gone forward with a trial. As it also turned out, his lack of understanding came close to costing him his high-income job. Fortunately for him, I was able to successfully have his guilty plea vacated after filing papers with the court. However, it is an uphill battle to convince a court to do so—he was just lucky. It could have very easily turned out differently for him. The bottom line is that people charged with DWI need to understand all of the consequences of pleading guilty or being found guilty after a trial.

BEST WAY TO DEFEND AGAINST A DWI

There's no simple "best way" to defend against a DWI or DUI because every arrest is a little bit different, though many have overall similarities. For instance, perhaps the driver performs poorly in the field sobriety test due to a 10 percent hearing loss that the officer didn't ask him about. Even if the driver fails all of the balancing tests, this may provide a good defense for the field sobriety test results.

An experienced DWI attorney will review the evidence and specific circumstances to find proper defenses, such as medications or dentures, which might affect breathalyzer results. However, as a DWI attorney, one of my other functions is to explain who my client is to the prosecutor and to the court. In other words, instead of my client just being a name on a criminal charge before the court and the prosecutor I "lift my client off the paper". Perhaps my client is a very good and honorable person who does a tremendous amount of work as a volunteer—someone who's won awards and accolades. These details often make a huge difference in plea negotiations.

For example, let's say my client is a 21-year-old kid is charged with a DWI and he got a speeding ticket for reaching 110 miles per hour on the highway. If this is all of the information that the court and prosecutor has about my client, things are not looking so great from the start. However, once the prosecutor and court learn that my client is at the top of his graduating class at college, he has been a volunteer at a soup kitchen for several years, and he holds down a full-time job, these facts can be a point of persuasion during plea negotiations.

Typically, in DWI cases, the prosecutor doesn't make any independent inquiries about the defendant's background other than checking for prior criminal convictions, so it's crucial for the defense attorney to lift that person off of the paper.

NO DEFENSE DOESN'T MEAN "NO ATTORNEY NECESSARY"

Sometimes, there aren't any defenses. Let's say one of the many excellent police officers stops a driver for swerving over the double yellow lines in the road multiple times, ran a stop sign, and stopped at a green light. The defense attorney reviews the file, and the evidence of guilt is overwhelming against the client. After he was asked to get out of the car, he fell down 10 times, he could only stand up by balancing himself on his car, he is belligerent, and, while cursing, he has slurred speech. The officer observed an open bottle of vodka sitting in the car and he also observed the driver drinking from the bottle, the defendant has red eyes, and is unable to respond in any way to the officer. The driver takes the breathalyzer and the result is twice the legal limit. This situation doesn't mean that the defendant should just walk into the courtroom and plead guilty. An experienced DWI attorney can weigh the possibilities and defense strategies and perhaps transition into mitigation of the circumstances. Perhaps the prosecutor believes that he or she has an iron-clad case; that there's really no possible defense and he or she wants to seek state prison time for the defendant. That's a tough situation for a defense attorney who now has to convince the prosecutor that a plea offer with prison time is inappropriate in this situation.

For instance, I had an alcoholic client, the nicest guy—he reminded me of Morgan Freeman. Even though he was a few years away from retiring from the post office, his only life-long run-in with the criminal justice system was a result of his alcoholism and DWIs. His alcoholism had cost him everything that was dear to him throughout his life, from his house to his family, who wanted nothing to do with him. He had no criminal history other than multiple DWI convictions.

When I first met with this client, he'd been on felony DWI probation for about a year and was facing his second felony DWI conviction. He'd joined AA and then went into a short in-patient program, but nothing worked. He was frightened about losing his post office pension if he went to jail. I told him that we would attack the case aggressively but that he would also have to join a long-term in-patient program, which he did. The judge was impressed and my client got restored back to probation, without jail time.

Unfortunately, the long-term program still wasn't enough, and he picked up his third felony DWI within a year's time. The judge told me in court, "Mr. Sachs, your client's in a tough spot; if he's convicted, he's going to state prison. This guy's gotten too much slack here, and now he's going to hang himself with it. I just can't let this slide." My client told me, "Dave, this is it for me. No pension. My life's over; I've already lost everything and now it looks like I am going to prison for a long time." Knowing that he had very little to no chance at being successful at trial and faced a stiff prison sentence if convicted, I coordinated with several different alcohol programs, with the Department of Probation, my client's probation officer, and even with the prosecutor. I got my client into a solid program and helped him figure out how to pay for it; the program was very expensive. He did exceptionally well in the program and moved his residence next to the probation department.

Even after successfully completing a very extensive, long-term, in-patient program, the judge still intended to send him to state prison. However, probation was impressed by my client's transformation. He had become a mentor to other people in the program because he was so successful in the treatment. What I really did was to buy time for my client, despite the pending criminal charges, so that he had time to make serious progress toward recovery. When we got to the plea offer, the judge said, "If you plead guilty, the prosecution wants a stiff prison sentence. But if you keep on doing what you're doing, I'll consider other options." When we appeared before the judge at sentencing, I gave a very impassioned plea for a sentence of probation with the support of his probation officer. Everyone told me that I had no shot. In the end, the judge agreed to sentence my client to probation again with no jail time. It was a very stunning and unexpected victory for my client. This came from mitigation, lifting my client off the paper to show him as a real human being and attacking the root of his problem: alcoholism.

WHAT TO LOOK FOR IN A DWI ATTORNEY

Most people search for a DWI lawyer on the internet these days and when they do, dozens of DWI lawyers will pop up. The tough part of this is how to decide which attorney is a good fit. The first thing to use in finding a good DWI lawyer is your gut instincts on the issue of trust. Trust begins with having a proper amount of time to talk to the lawyer so you can ask a lot of questions and get to know the lawyer a little better so you can get a preview into how the attorney thinks and acts. Also, it will provide the client with an opportunity to learn what the attorney's experience and background consist of and whether the attorney instills confidence in the client in order to decide that the attorney is a good fit.

Sometimes, a person's gut instinct tells them, "I like this guy, but my instincts say that his personality isn't a good fit for me. He seems to know what he's doing, but I need someone whom I can understand when he talks to me. I want to have a good working relationship with my attorney." So, I encourage clients, even when they call for the first time, "Don't just trust what I'm telling you. Give yourself an opportunity to call around to other defense attorneys. Get a good feeling for who's out there and the choices that you have. Then make your selection."

After clients retain me, they often tell me one of the reasons that they did so was that I gave them a lot of time on telephone discussing their case with them without charging them any money and that during the conversation, I convinced them that I have a sound understanding of the law.

IN THE LONG RUN

Over the years, I receive a lot of calls asking about how to remove a previous DWI conviction from their record. While some states have expungement laws, New York State is not one of them. If you have a criminal conviction in New York State, it stays on your record for life. It's not coming off. While other states do have expungement laws, those states often make exceptions for DWI charges. So the conviction will stay on your record for the rest of your life.

Remember, if you are charged with a DWI it's essential to know the collateral consequences of a criminal conviction before you plead guilty or go to trial.

128

BENCH OR JURY TRIAL

If you're charged with a misdemeanor or felony in New York, you have the unassailable right to have a jury decide your fate at a trial, or you can have a bench trial in which a judge sits at the trial of fact instead of a jury. In other words, if you have a bench trial, you essentially have only one juror to hear the case: the judge. If the defendant wants either a bench trial or a jury trial, it's his or her right as an accused person to make that choice. The judge can't stop it. The prosecutor can't stop it. It's going to happen. Laws regarding the right of the accused to a bench trial will vary from state to state. However, in general, they follow the same standards as those found in the state of New York.

When a client is approaching a trial, I sit down to discuss the decision to have a bench trial or jury trial extensively with my client. It can be a tricky choice. There are reasons to have a jury and there are reasons not to have a jury. This is the short explanation: when cases are very fact-based, it's always good to have a jury. This principle applies to any criminal defense situation.

Since judges are usually attorneys, they understand the law. Whenever the legal issues are based more upon the law itself rather than on tangible facts, it might be wise to have a judge try the case. So the question goes beyond just flipping a coin to decide if you want a jury over the bench trial. It's not a simple question to answer. There is huge amount of analysis involved in the decision-making process that could only be properly examined, explained, and reviewed by an attorney with the client. This especially applies if it's a person's first offense, like an everyday driver charged with DWI. They won't understand those nuances and they won't understand the law. They won't understand how to dissect whether this is a case that's entirely factual (which lends itself to a jury) or a case that involves more details of the law (which should be tried before a judge).

Another big issue, which should influence the decision, centers on the habits of the judge and your attorney's knowledge of the judge's reputation and background with bench trials. Maybe the judge convicts everybody at bench trials and acts like a second prosecutor in the courtroom. It might never be a good idea to have a bench trial with a specific judge. Sometimes the complete opposite is true. Perhaps this judge is very fair-minded and reasonable. He or she analyzes and deliberates thoroughly over the evidence and relevant circumstances.

THE VERY BEST DEFENSE

Even though this may sound ridiculously simplistic, the best defense for any DWI is not to drink and drive. This goes back to my comment that I'm fully in favor of tough DWI laws. However, in the real world, I understand that even good and honorable people make mistakes. It isn't always some drunk on a binge. No matter who you are, even if you're not a big drinker, anyone can be charged with DWI. This can include people with very different backgrounds such as doctors, lawyers, teachers, carpenters, plumbers, accountants, sales associates, etc.

People often come into my office after facing a charge of DWI for the first time. As one of my clients told me, "I'm 50 years old. I'm a professional. I've never been in trouble all my life— never even had a parking ticket. I'm out to dinner with friends. I only had a couple of glasses of wine. I thought I was fine. I got in the car, and I got pulled over. Bam! Next thing I know, I'm charged with DWI. I can't believe this is happening to me."

It's really tough for any person to know with any accuracy the level of alcohol in his or her system. People often think that they can know when they're sober. So they say, "Yes, I can have a couple of drinks and still be sober." Then they go out to dinner and get engrossed in conversation. Even if they've had four glasses of wine, they think, "I've only had a few glasses. Maybe I had two or three after the whole meal is said and done." Maybe they're not paying attention, and then they ask themselves, "Hey, am I good to drive?" They conclude that they are in a good enough state to drive. They don't FEEL drunk.

Let me just say that it's not the best time to be asking yourself whether you're good to drive after drinking alcohol. The time to ask yourself that particular question is before you go out and drink. Say to yourself, "After a few glasses of wine, I don't think that I'm going to be in a position to understand whether or not I'm okay to drive." That's why the best defense is to drink responsibly without deciding to drink and drive. Prepare by scheduling a designated driver, or arrange for some alternative means for getting back home. When they are drinking, people are always the worst judges of their own driving ability.

In a recent case of mine, my client was driving from Vermont to the Carolinas and had an accident in New York. This fifty-year-old man is an alcoholic who has been in and out of rehab throughout his entire life and had trouble keeping jobs. He'd been drinking bottle after bottle of vodka since he left Vermont, stopping on the side of the road to sleep for short periods of time. At some point, he wakes up and discovers that he is out of alcohol. He stops at a gas station or liquor store to buy more vodka or beer. Lo and behold, during one of those stops in New York, he gets into an accident. The client doesn't even remember that he got off at the exit. As he was driving, he blacked out on the highway and crashed his car into a stop sign.

Unfortunately, there are alcoholics driving on the road at this very minute. Unless and until the alcoholics get proper treatment for their disease, they'll be on the road. While DWI is not completely preventable in a general sense, DWI is very preventable for the individual who drinks responsibly. It's even preventable for the alcoholic if he or she obtains the proper treatment.

It sounds contradictory to some people to say that I'm in favor of tough DWI laws. However, I have children, a wife, and a family (like my brother-in-law, Ken Manse, who took my picture which appears on the back of this book). I have a big family and we're out there on the road together all the time. When I hear horror stories about accidents, about innocent people getting killed by alcoholics on the road, I don't react any differently than anybody else. I'm shocked and sickened. Working as a DWI attorney doesn't make me immune from these realities. I don't want these people on the road. Believe it or not, when my DWI clients walk in, I talk to them about the danger that they pose to others. I consider it a duty to discourage my clients from drinking and driving. I urge problem drinkers to get help. I want to discourage drunk driving just like I want to discourage crime. Yet, in all events, I make sure that my clients receive the legal defense and protections that they are guaranteed by our Constitution. This is how our system works. This is the law and the law must be applied equally to all of us, whether we are guilty or innocent.

(This content should be used for informational purposes only. It does not create an attorney-client relationship with any reader and should not be construed as legal advice. If you need legal

advice, please contact an attorney in your community who can assess the specifics of your situation.)

6

IS THERE ANY HOPE OF AVOIDING CONVICTION?

by R. Shane Herzner, Esq.

R. Shane Herzner, Esq.
Herzner Law, LLC
Cincinnati, Ohio
www.herznerlaw.com

Shane Herzner is a former Hamilton County Assistant Prosecutor. As an Assistant Prosecutor, Mr. Herzner represented the State of Ohio in numerous cases including OVI/DUI/DWI, License Suspensions, Domestic Violence, Theft, and various other Misdemeanor and Felony matters. In 2008, Mr. Herzner left the Prosecutor's Office to practice Criminal Defense work.

*As a Defense Attorney, Mr. Herzner has aggressively repre-
sented clients in hundreds of cases and was recently named a
Rising Star by Super Lawyers Magazine (2013).*

*Mr. Herzner is certified in the training for the National Highway
Traffic Safety Administration (NHTSA) and the International
Association of Chiefs of Police (IACP), DWI Detention and
Standardized Field Sobriety Testing (Student Course). He also
regularly attends the most advanced OVI/DUI/DWI seminars to
stay up on the latest testing machines and case law.*

IS THERE ANY HOPE OF
AVOIDING CONVICTION?

You are not required to take the field sobriety tests. If you have
been stopped for suspicion of driving under the influence, I
recommend that you don't take any of the standardized field
sobriety tests or any other roadside tests. If you do take the tests
but don't do well, your willingness to be tested will not help you
to avoid the conviction. Further, several factors may affect your
ability to perform the standardized field sobriety tests. Perhaps
you have an ongoing knee injury, a recurrent back injury, or a
head injury. Age, location, and weather conditions can also
affect the results of the test.

For example, if you are taking the tests on the side of a highway
with trucks driving by at 65 mph and flashing strobe lights in
your face, you will not do nearly as well as if you were taking
the tests in an air-conditioned hotel—or at the academy where
law enforcement officers learn to administer field sobriety tests.
Roadside tests are not controlled. In many cases, at an actual

arrest, the environment of the standardized field sobriety tests was not controlled. However, just because a person takes the tests and doesn't do well on them doesn't spell the end of the world; many explanations can be given to a judge or a jury for a poor result on the tests. Remember that you will not lose your license because you didn't take the tests.

STANDARDIZED FIELD SOBRIETY TESTS

There are three standardized field sobriety tests approved by the National Highway Traffic Safety Administration (NHTSA) for alcohol impairment. The first one is known as the Horizontal Gaze Nystagmus test; it's commonly referred to as the 'pen test' because you follow a stimulus with your eyes as the officer moves it across your field of vision and shines a flashlight in your eyes. Another is the Walk-and-Turn test; you walk, heel-to-toe, nine steps, turn, and take nine steps back. The third standardized field sobriety test is the One-Leg Stand test; you stand on one leg, hold the other leg approximately six inches above the ground, and count. This is a 30-second test timed by the officer.

As you can see, two of these field sobriety tests (the One-Leg Stand and the Walk-and-Turn) are based on a person's physical ability to balance. I have noticed that during the Walk-and-Turn test, most people do not walk heel-to-toe. The officer may make a very general statement such as, "Hey, you can walk a line, can't you?" Most people can walk a straight line when they are walking normally; however, if you ask that person to walk on a straight line heel-to-toe they may have difficulty because that is an unnatural way to walk. No one walks that way. The officer may ask, "Why don't you want to do the field test when you just have to walk a line?" That is not an accurate depiction of what you are going to be doing.

Standardized field sobriety tests are just that, standardized. In other words, the test should be administered with the exact same instructions, whether you are in Ohio or California. While officers are performing the standardized field sobriety tests, especially the two physical ones, they are looking for clues exhibited during these tests. On the Walk-and-Turn test, among other clues, they are looking to see if you raise your arms more than six inches from your side, if you touch heel-to-toe on each step, and if you take nine steps. For the turn, you take a series of small steps to turn around instead of pivoting.

In many cases, I find that the officer has failed to instruct the driver or passenger on some of the cues or clues that he is looking for during the test. He is required to tell the person to "keep your arms down at your side during the entire test, walk heel-to-toe, take the nine steps, then turn." Sometimes he will forget specific instructions but still mark you down for cues or clues. This is another example—when you are in the starting position, you are supposed to maintain that position until the officer tells you to start the test. Many times, the officer will forget to give that instruction, or prior to giving that instruction, the person will stand in a more natural position while listening to the officer's instructions. The officer then marks down a clue against that person because he did not stand in the correct position during the instructions, even before he performed any portion of that particular test.

I do not believe that these tests are reliable, not only because of police officer error in giving instructions, but also because I don't think that people generally perform well on these tests, given the performance-affecting roadside complications such as nerves or a medical condition. Most people are incredibly nervous, especially if they know that they have had some alcohol, when they get stopped by a police officer and are asked to exit the car. Then they are supposed to perform a test, knowing that if they do not do well, they may be spending the night in jail. Most people will be incredibly nervous when taking these field sobriety tests.

None of the other tests (i.e. the Alphabet test, the Number test, Touching-Your-Finger-to-Your-Nose) are standardized field sobriety tests to determine impairment. In other words, no scientific evidence shows that you're impaired if you cannot say the alphabet backwards or count backwards from 68 to 53. So why even take these tests, since they will only make you look stupid? Also, the officer and the prosecutor will use these tests against you and say, "Look, you couldn't even say the alphabet backwards," even if there is not a single scientific study indicating that this test is an accurate indicator of impairment.

There is no reason in the world to perform a non-standardized field sobriety test. As with most tests, unless you practice, you won't do well at them; so, there's no real incentive to do any of the standardized or non-standardized field tests.

Even if you pass the non-standardized tests, the officer and prosecutor will say, "These non-standardized tests don't have anything to do with a person's ability to operate a motor vehicle." I could not agree with them more, but they only say that when it is to their benefit. You will not lose anything, not even your license, for not taking the roadside field sobriety tests, because they are strictly optional. There is nothing about the implied consent laws that require you to take roadside tests. However, there are different implications with the breath test and losing your license.

CHEMICAL TESTS

A refusal to be tested on the official state breath/blood/urine instrument means that you will lose your license. Ohio, perhaps all states, have an implied consent law which essentially states that if you are requested by law enforcement officers to take a chemical test, either you take it or you lose your license. Each state has its own rules as far as the length of license suspension; Ohio law requires a first-time offender in six years who refuses to take a chemical test be given a one-year suspension. If you do take a chemical test (either breath, blood, or urine) and fail it, in each of the 50 states, you will lose your license as part of the implied consent. In Ohio, a first-time offender within a six-year time frame will lose their license for one year for refusing to take a chemical test and 90 days for failing a chemical test.

In my opinion, there are times when a person should submit to a chemical test and times when they should not submit to a chemical test. The majority of the time, I recommend that people refuse to take a breath test, partially because the officer can arrest you on the scene for a charge of driving under the influence (DUI) or operating a vehicle impaired (OVI). In other words, the officer will place you in handcuffs and inform you that you have been placed under arrest on-scene for the officer's opinion-based DUI. After he takes you back to the police station for an official chemical test, knowing that you have already been placed under arrest, he will give you an option to take a breath test.

If you take and fail the chemical test, you will get charged with a second violation of the OVI or DUI statute ("failing a chemical test".) For first-time offenders, by taking that chemical test, you actually are creating a second charge for yourself, a *per se* violation; whereas, if you refuse to take the breath test at the scene, you only have to overcome the opinion-based portion of the OVI. On the other hand, if you have any prior convictions and refuse to take a breath test, they can charge you for refusing to take a breath test while having a prior conviction, which may bring some added consequences as far as mandatory minimum penalties. Keep this in mind, in Ohio an OVI is an enhanceable offense where the penalties could increase if you refuse to take the breath test and have a prior conviction or if you fail a chemical test and have had a prior conviction in the past six years.

In general, I advise people to refuse to take the breath test; the only time that I recommend taking a breath test is if the person has had no alcohol, or if he has positively had only one drink and will be under the legal limit. The officer must make the determination to arrest you whether you are above a 0.08 or not because impairment and being over the *per se* level are two completely different things. Sometimes people will come into my office and say, "Hey, I felt fine, but I drink all the time and I didn't think that I was impaired." Remember that the officer does not need to prove impairment if you take the breath test; he just needs to show that you were over the 0.08 limit.

Unfortunately, in Ohio and around the country, if you refuse a breath test, some judges are a bit more hesitant to grant driving privileges. You are still allowed to request driving privileges after a certain amount of hard suspension time. Therefore, I think it is important to call an attorney before taking a breath test at the police station, so you know your jurisdiction and the possible ramifications of that refusal beyond just a license suspension. A local attorney should know the preferences of the court system in these types of cases, in addition to the general trend of ruling by the judges in that jurisdiction.

Now, if you do refuse to take a breath test, that refusal will be used against you in court. In Ohio, the prosecutor will present the common assumption to the jury in the form of a question—why would anyone who is under the legal limit refuse to take a breath test? Obviously, the argument on the defense side is the opposite—why wouldn't you refuse? If you're already under arrest, the breath test does you absolutely no good. Each year, I probably represent five or six people who have tested under the legal limit but have already been arrested for the impairment section at the scene. In my eyes, I see no benefit to taking a chemical test. That is more of a trial strategy rather than trying to decide at the scene whether or not to take a test. Opinion arrests can be beat; numbers or facts can be much more difficult to defeat. Failing a field sobriety test or refusing a test can be used against you in court, but there are ways that you can explain the results or reasoning to the judge or jury.

WHAT IS A MIRANDA WARNING?

Miranda warnings are legally required to be read to you if the police officer plans to interrogate you. If the officer does not read you the Miranda warning, that oversight does not mean that your case will be automatically thrown out. It means that any of your post-arrest statements cannot be used during the trial. Nine times out of ten, if Miranda is not read out, the officer does not ask many questions; he believes that he has already gathered the necessary evidence to arrest you for the

OVI or the DUI at the scene or at the station. Even though officers may not ask many questions, most of the time they do read out the Miranda warning; it's just their policy to always read it after arrest. I cannot tell you the number of times that clients have arrived at my office and said, "Hey, my case can be thrown out, I wasn't read Miranda."

However, that has nothing at all to do with the DUI; Miranda only pertains to statements that you may or may not have made after the arrest. "What do I say and do if I am confronted by a police officer and suspected of DUI/DWI?" I always advise that less is more; it's best to say as little as possible during an interaction with the police officer. Remember that you are not under arrest at that point, so Miranda does not need to be read. Any statements that you make to the officer can be used against you, including an admission to drinking, the number of drinks, your previous location and its purpose, such as whether or not you were at a bar or a company party.

When you are stopped, before the officer comes up to the car, it is always a good idea to keep your driver's license out and ready to hand to him. As he approaches the car, he will already be making observations. For example, he will look to see if you fumble with your license, have difficulty pulling it out of your wallet, or have difficulty finding the license. Often, especially if you have never been stopped before, you will be incredibly nervous as you wait for the police officer to come to the window because you know that you have consumed some alcohol. You may show some signs of impairment, even if you are not impaired, simply due to nerves. However, even though you must answer the officer's questions about your name and your residence, you are not legally required to answer questions about your previous whereabouts and the amount that you have had to drink. I recommend that you say, "Officer, before I answer any of those questions, I would like to talk to an attorney."

I know it sounds a little hokey, but it is in your best interests not to answer any questions; if you do answer questions, under no circumstances should you lie. In other words, if you have had something to drink, do not tell him that you have not had anything to drink. It is better to not answer that question at all than to say no and be proven wrong, because if a judge or jury later hears that you were dishonest, they will not believe any of your other statements during that time period. If the officer requests that you get out of the car, you do have to get out of the car, but you do not have to perform any of the tests. As attorneys, we recommend that you not perform any of the tests, and that you don't answer any additional questions. If the officer makes the decision to arrest you at that point, he will have very little evidence to offer as proof for a conviction. Again, less is better. If you offer very little, you have a better chance at prevailing in your case.

ARE THERE CRIMINAL PENALTIES FOR REFUSING TESTING?

Yes and no, depending on your jurisdiction. For a first DUI in Ohio, since each state has its own mandatory minimums, a refusal does not enhance your first DUI conviction. A refusal only enhances the mandatory minimum penalties if there are prior DUIs. For an initial DUI, there are no additional criminal penalties. If you are convicted of a refusal, enhanced penalties can be applied.

Do You Have The Right Of Counsel Before Agreeing Or Refusing To Submit To The State's Test?

That is a little tricky. As I always recommend, you can ask for an attorney. However, the problem is that the police officer will say, "Okay, call your attorney." Most people are not planning to get stopped for a DUI, so they do not have the name or phone number of a DUI attorney in their telephone; most people are not prepared for that questions and do not know who to call. When the officer hands you a phone book, you will have to call a random attorney that you do not know. You do have the right to request the advice of an attorney, but unless you know an attorney who you can call, it can be very difficult.

Also, there's another problem to face—you will probably not be able to connect with an attorney when you call his or her office. Now, I am always available, and I have received phone calls from clients who have asked me questions regarding whether or not to take a breath test; this is not uncommon. However, the overwhelming majority of DUI offenders are first-time offenders, so a DUI attorney never sees them again after the first charge.

Most of the time, I tell people that they can also say, "Look, I'm going to talk to my attorney before I take your field sobriety test." In my experience, the officer will not give you the opportunity to call an attorney. In most cases, the officer will say, "Now, if you can't do my test, I'm just going to place you under arrest." If an officer makes you get out of the vehicle because he smells alcohol, he will probably arrest you. It's very rare that I hear a story about someone taking a field sobriety test without being charged for a DUI, or someone passing the test and being allowed to go on their merry way. Those instances are very few and far between.

IF YOU REQUEST AN INDEPENDENT TEST, MUST THE OFFICER ACCOMMODATE THAT REQUEST?

No, the officer is not required to accommodate a reasonable request for an independent test. However, on Ohio's implied consent form, it does say that you can have an independent test—at your own expense. Most of the time, this statement means that after your arrest, you can go to a hospital to take an independent blood test. Unfortunately, hospitals are reluctant to do blood draws because of the medical malpractice suits; therefore, just know that the process can be difficult. Nurses are required to do blood draws, and they do not like to do blood draws for people just to serve as an independent source of evidence. It takes up their time, and they would much rather handle emergency room patients or people with "real emergencies." If you think that you are under the alcohol limit but you did not take the breath test, and you can get the blood test done at a hospital within Ohio's required three-hour period, absolutely get it done. It's difficult, like having an attorney's phone number on hand and also getting through to him, but it's a good way to protect yourself.

As a matter of fact, the law enforcement officer gets to pick the type of chemical test. If you have already been placed under arrest at the scene, then you take a breath test and it shows that you're under the 0.08 limit, the officer can request that you do a blood or urine test; he may suspect that you are under the influence of drugs instead of alcohol. At that point, he can theoretically request that you take all three chemical tests. If you refuse any one of these chemical tests, it is counted against you as a refusal. That is one of the reasons why I suggest most of the time that people are better off refusing to take chemical tests.

What Do You Think Is The Most Reliable And Accurate Form Of Testing?

I do not have a lot of confidence in breath testing machines because there are so many outside elements that could cause inaccurate results. In Ohio, we cannot attack the general reliability of a breath-testing machine. If one of my clients uses an expert witness during a trial, that expert witness cannot testify to the fact that these machines are unreliable. He can only testify about that specific machine and the specific characteristics that my client possesses that may have caused an errant test. For example, if you suffer from gastroesophageal reflux disease (GERD), that could have an effect on the accuracy of the machine. If you have been drinking, due to the residual alcohol, dentures can have an effect on the accuracy of a breath test, so you should remove the dentures before doing the breath test. Operator error can also cause a false high reading on breath tests. Even your cell phone, through radio frequency interference, can cause the machine to give inaccurate results.

In my opinion, the worst chemical test is the urine test, because urine concentration is unreliable. If you have held your urine for a long time, obviously the concentration of alcohol will be much greater than if you frequently used the restroom that evening. I have seen the results of breath tests in which a person tested under the limit in multiple breath tests, so the officer had him do urine test, convinced that he must be under the influence of drugs. That urine test was tested at a rate almost twice as high as the blood alcohol content (BAC) level displayed by the breath test. The difference is based on how frequently the person visited the bathroom. I definitely would not agree to a urine test.

If you had to pick out one particular test, a blood test would probably be the most accurate. However, several things come into play even with a blood test. For instance, if an alcohol swab was used on your skin prior to drawing the blood, that could have a little bit of an effect on your results. If you were involved in a very serious accident, that could also have an effect on your BAC level. Out of the three chemical tests, I would say that a blood test is probably the most reliable and the most accurate because it really tests the alcohol content in your blood at its source.

How Can I Find A Qualified DUI Attorney?

Most of the time, I recommend that people ask a friend for an attorney referral. Talking to friends or relatives whom an attorney has represented is a good method because it gives you a good idea of the level of quality in the job done by the attorney. Secondly, try calling an attorney that you already know, or who has represented you before, and ask him or her for a recommendation of a qualified DUI attorney who will do a good job.

The Internet is another good resource; you can research an attorney to find out a little bit about the attorney's experience, their type of work, and their clients' testimonials on their website. Also, it's important to meet with your attorney before hiring him, if you can. It may be difficult because first hearings are set so quickly, and you should normally hire an attorney prior to going to court. If that's not possible because of time restraints, it is always best just to say, "I'm not guilty," and contact an attorney as soon as possible. I cannot stress that enough. Many times, I've spoken with clients who said, "Hey, I hired my attorney over the phone. I haven't heard back from him since I hired him. Do I need to find another attorney?" This is why I do not think that it's a good idea to hire an attorney over the phone unless it is absolutely necessary.

It's also good to develop a personal relationship with your attorney. The only way that you will know if an attorney will work for you is if you meet him face to face. For me, the worst thing is to meet a client at court for the first time. If the attorney takes the time to meet with you before you hire him, he will also take the time to call you and follow up on important case matters. Personal contact with the attorney is so incredibly important.

If you do not get the feeling that that attorney will work for you, you can always set up additional appointments to meet with additional attorneys. When you meet with the attorney, ask good questions and evaluate his answers. It is like an interview process. You are interviewing that attorney to find out if he is the one that you want to help with your case; in my opinion, the client is the boss. I only make recommendations. The client pays my fee and ultimately makes the decision on how to go forward with the case.

What Kind Of Questions Should I Ask When Meeting A Lawyer For The First Time?

It is always good to review the mandatory minimum penalties. You need to ask, "What are the penalties for a conviction?" and "What are the future consequences of the conviction?" For example, a DUI is considered a serious offense in Canada, so you could have serious issues crossing the Canadian border after receiving a DUI conviction. You must petition the Canadian consulate if you want to enter Canada within a certain time period after a DUI conviction. This is one of the unintended consequences of a DUI conviction that people often don't even realize.

Second, ask the attorney, "What are the other consequences besides the criminal penalties? How can this affect my future?" Certainly ask about the DUI's possible effect on your job. "Will this affect my ability to keep my nursing license or my teaching certificate?" If the attorney is skilled in DUI matters, he should be able to answer these questions because he has represented clients who have asked these very same questions.

Third, ask the attorney about their success rate with DUI cases. "How often do you try DUI cases? How often do you prevail when you do try DUI cases? How many trials have you had before this particular court or this particular judge? What has been your experience with this particular court or with this particular judge?" In some courts, these answers do become an important factor when talking about pre-negotiations. If the attorney is familiar with the court and familiar with the judge, he may be able to offer a better idea of a reasonable expectation. The attorney may not be able to tell you, "You're going to win your case," but he can tell you, "Based on our conversations, this is my opinion on the strengths and weaknesses of your case."

Building a relationship with your attorney, asking him questions about his success rate and the number of times that he has tried cases, is incredibly important. If you are paying a substantial amount of money to an attorney who never takes cases to trial, that can mean one of two things: either he is not a very good trial attorney or he is so good that the prosecuting attorney does not want to deal with him.

HOW WOULD AN ATTORNEY HELP ME GET A BETTER OFFER ON MY CASE?

I was a prosecutor for Hamilton County for several years. During my time there, I could have told you which attorneys tried cases and which attorneys did not try cases. The attorneys who tried cases negotiated much better plea deals than non-trial attorneys, because I had no incentive as a prosecutor to offer a deal to their client. If I knew that the attorney was a good attorney who also tried cases, more often than not, that attorney would get an even better plea deal because I would have to spend my afternoon or my day dealing with that well-prepared defense attorney who would do a good job for his client. The attorneys who are prepared and willing to go to court will get the best plea deals, no matter where they practice.

PLEA OR TRIAL: HOW DO I PREPARE FOR BOTH?

I generally take a case in stages. The first stage is a meeting with the client, finding out the client's immediate need. What type of driving privileges does he need? Can I waive his appearance because his presence at court is keeping him from work? One of the most important reasons to hire an attorney is to keep your job. During the first stage, I find out the client's best interests regarding the case. In our meetings, I ask clients a lot of questions about their type of work and their family life so that I can personalize their case; I get a good idea about what I am facing prior to reviewing the facts of the case.

Second, in the discovery phase, I try to gather as much information as possible so that the client can make a good, educated decision on the way to proceed with his case. If there is a plea offer on the table at any point in the process, I always take it to the client whether it is early or late in the case, just so the client knows the status or level of progress in the case. It is important to keep communication lines open.

Once we get all of the information, such as police reports and investigation notes for discovery, I send the client copies to review. After he has reviewed the information, we meet again in the office to examine the information. Also, if there is a video or cruiser cam, I bring a client in to review that in person. I will point out case strengths and weaknesses and offer the client my opinion as to the possibility of prevailing. This is one of those gray areas, not black-and-white, because you cannot treat each client in the exact same way, especially when it comes to deciding whether to offer a plea or go to trial. So, after the client comes to my office and reviews everything, he ultimately makes the decision whether to take the case to trial or to work toward a pretrial plea bargain. What may be good for one client may not be good for another. For example, if my client does a lot of driving and cannot have a DUI on his record, we may have to try the case if the prosecutor is not willing to work with us on a pretrial plea bargain.

That is why there is more of an individualized response than simply, "Yes, I always litigate cases when this happens," or, "I know how to litigate a case when this happens." I have litigated breath cases that seemed to be very difficult to defend, and we won at the trial. On the other hand, very rarely, I have pleaded out some cases at arraignment. One client had a very personal need to get the driver's license right away, and we were able to do that at the arraignment. The best thing to do is to gather all the information, present it to a client, present the options, and then make a recommendation. The client must then determine what is in his or her best interests for that particular situation.

WHY SHOULD YOU DEFEND A GUILTY PERSON?

I always take the approach that I do not know whether the person is innocent or guilty. For one thing, my serious doubts concerning breath testing keep me from saying, "Those kids over there are guilty," because many factors come into play with chemical tests. Second, it is not up to me to decide on a person's innocence or guilt. It is up to me to collect all of the information and present it to a judge or a jury, so they can make that decision. It is not a matter of guilt or no guilt, or whether you are guilty or innocent; it is a matter of presenting the evidence in the best way for the client and zealously representing the client.

DUI defense is slightly different from some other types of crimes that the person either committed or didn't commit because most DUIs are opinion-based. I do not have any issues sleeping at night, knowing that I am attacking an opinion. The innocence or guilt is always left to the jury or the judge. This is the process of the legal system—a judge or jury, after looking at all the facts, makes the determination of innocence or guilt.

People believe that there are more drunken drivers on the road during holidays like New Year's Eve. My experience is that DUIs come about when people do not plan ahead. No one plans to get a DUI. When you plan to go out to a New Year's Eve party, knowing you will be having a few drinks, make transportation arrangements. Pick a designated driver, plan to take a taxi, or find another way to get home from the party.

More often than not, the person who went to a company happy hour or an office party planned to have maybe one or two drinks, but ended up having that third drink. Therefore, those people do not necessarily plan on drinking a lot of alcohol, but

154

just staying that extra hour or hanging out with a friend a little bit longer because of a stressful day added to their alcohol consumption. This is why we see many cases of first-time offenders; they were not planning to drink as much as they did, and they did not have a plan in place to get home after drinking.

In my experience, once a person has been arrested for a DUI, any time in the future that he has alcohol to drink, he is already making plans to get home. My advice is this: just do not drink and drive at all. One of my friends often says, "I've never seen a bar that doesn't have an outside parking lot." After a person goes through the horrific experience and collateral damage of being charged with a DUI (such as paying reinstatement fees and court costs and attending a driver's intervention program), that person generally makes very good future decisions about how much to drink and whether to drive afterwards.

WHAT ARE THE CONSEQUENCES OR PENALTIES ASSOCIATED WITH A DUI, AND HOW LONG DOES DUI STAY ON YOUR RECORD?

Although a DUI carries criminal consequences such as jail time, it is still classified as a traffic offense *per se*. If someone checks your traffic record, he or she will see the DUI; like all traffic offenses in Ohio, it stays forever on the record, and never gets expunged. For the purposes of insurance or DMV points, yes, there is a look-back period. Most of the time, I believe that this period spans three years for insurance companies and two years for DMV purposes.

As far as consequences for DUI convictions, most jurisdictions and states have mandatory minimum penalties for jail time, or they offer a driver's intervention program. There is always a mandatory minimum license suspension. In Ohio, a first-time offense requires a suspension between six months to three years. The court could also order an interlock device to be placed in your car, requiring you to blow into the device prior to starting the car. In Ohio, you may also be required to get restrictive plates, which are brightly-colored plates for DUI offenders. Plates are generally not given to first-time offenders, but instead are required for multiple offenders (depending on the timeline of the priors convictions). This adds a social stigma that often comes with a DUI conviction. Ohio also has mandatory minimum fines and jail time in addition to license reinstatement fees, if your license is suspended. If you are required to attend a driver's intervention program, you must pay probation fees. Of course, you must pay your attorney as well.

In Ohio, a first-time convicted DUI offender is facing a $475 reinstatement fee, approximately $500 for the driver's intervention program, plus a mandatory minimum fine from $375 up to $1,075, besides court costs. The total comes to about $1,500 before payments to the attorney. In cases of a more restrictive suspension, you may also have to pay the cost of an interlock device and taxis when you cannot quickly get back your driving privileges. In Ohio, if a person hires a competent DUI attorney, the total cost will be somewhere in the range of at least $4,000 to $10,000 for a first-time offense.

The most important thing that I can do is educate people on their rights regarding a DUI charge. Otherwise, how will people know that they do not have to perform standardized field sobriety tests? I want to try to impart as much knowledge as possible to people concerning what to do at a DUI stop; the more you know, the better your chances are of not being arrested, or fighting your case so that you prevail. Educating people before they get into trouble is so incredibly important. Many clients come to see me and tell me, "Geez, man, I wish I would have known that before I got arrested." I wish I could have told them this information before they were arrested. This is one avenue where we have to educate people about their rights as well as what to do (or not do) when stopped by a police officer.

(This content should be used for informational purposes only. It does not create an attorney-client relationship with any reader and should not be construed as legal advice. If you need legal advice, please contact an attorney in your community who can assess the specifics of your situation.)

7

THE COMPONENTS OF EFFECTIVE DUI DEFENSE IN VIRGINIA

by Mark R. Matney, Esq.

Mark R. Matney, Esq.

Matney Law, PLLC
Newport News, Virginia
www.newportnewsduiattorney.net

Mark R. Matney is a traffic defense lawyer who regularly represents clients charged with DUI and reckless driving. He is a member of the National College for DUI Defense. He attained a Certificate of Competency in the Basic Science of Evidential Breath Alcohol Testing by completing training with one of the leading breath machine manufacturers. He is a member of the Virginia State Bar, the National College for DUI Defense, and the Newport News Bar Association.

Besides graduating from William and Mary's Marshall Wythe School of Law, he has completed his B.A. in international studies at The American University and his M.Div. degree having graduated summa cum laude from Evangel Theological Seminary.

He is also active in his community and has donated over 450 hours of volunteer legal services through the Alliance Defending Freedom. He has served on the boards of a local ministry and a seminary, and instructed for Evangel Theological Seminary.

THE COMPONENTS OF EFFECTIVE DUI DEFENSE IN VIRGINIA

PLEA BARGAIN OR TRIAL?

For most people, their first concern is to find a lawyer who will fight for them and not just plea bargain their case away. Some prospective clients tell me that they are concerned about lawyers who promise to "get them a deal" and others confide that they have experienced negative situations where they felt their prior lawyer pushed them into a plea agreement instead of helping with their cases. In other words, the idea of plea bargaining has a very bad connotation for many people. They believe that if their attorney enters into a plea bargain, he is not adequately representing his client. As a lawyer, I feel that my job is to obtain the best possible result for my client and that I need to explore all of the options, including both going to trial and negotiating with the prosecution.

When I accept a case, I become responsible for the zealous representation of my client. My staff and I research the facts and the legal issues and I inform my clients of our findings. My counsel includes discussing the risks of accepting an offer from the prosecution versus the risks of going to trial. I advise my clients that there is a risk involved regardless of whether they choose to negotiate a result with the prosecutor (a plea bargain) or to present the case to the judge. Going to trial means giving up the best offer from the prosecutor and risking a worse result from the judge. On the other hand, accepting the prosecutor's best offer means losing the possibility of a better result at trial.

Sometimes the focus of a case must be on avoiding a worse result as compared to "winning" or achieving a lesser charge. For example, one of my clients was charged with DUI because he fell asleep in the drive-thru lane at a fast food restaurant. When the police officer approached him, he saw that my client had vomited on himself and that he had receipts in his car for a large quantity of alcohol. There were numerous complicating factors in this case, including being assigned to a judge who was known for dealing harshly with DUI cases. I spoke with the officer to explore the option of going to trial and then discussed the situation with my client. The officer agreed that if we pled guilty to the DUI, he would not inform the judge of the aggravating factors: vomiting on himself, waking up with difficulty, performing poorly on field tests, and possessing receipts in his vehicle for large quantities of alcohol. When I explained the situation to my client he approved accepting the agreement instead of risking a trial. The end result that morning was a DUI without any of the enhanced penalties that would have been likely if the police officer had described the details of what he observed during the arrest. Although it is not as exciting as a trial, an agreement that avoids the risk of a more severe outcome may be the best result that can be accomplished in a particular case.

Another example of the challenge of deciding whether to negotiate a resolution or to go to trial can be seen in a case that involved an unusual medical defense. My client was charged with a first offense DUI with a blood alcohol content (BAC) of 0.15, which is almost twice the legal limit of 0.08. The 0.15 BAC triggers a five-day mandatory minimum jail sentence when someone is found guilty. As we prepared for trial, we received an offer from the prosecutor to amend the BAC so that my client would avoid any jail time. Although the offer of avoiding a jail sentence without the risk of a trial was tempting, my client chose to proceed to trial instead of accepting the prosecutor's offer. At the conclusion of the trial, the judge expressed his agreement with our medical expert and ruled that my client was not guilty of DUI. In hindsight, it is clear that the client made the best decision for his case. However, when the decision to reject the offer was made, there was no guarantee that we would prevail at trial. In fact, another client with a similar medical defense lost her case with a different judge, despite a lower BAC.

It is not always easy to decide whether the plea bargain or the trial is the best option. The plea agreement can sometimes sound very inviting. The prosecutor may offer to dismiss additional charges or to agree to a favorable sentence. As attorneys, we use all of the information available to us to provide the best counsel to our clients. Ultimately, however, clients must decide whether to risk the unknown result of a trial or accept the certainty of an agreement with the prosecution.

PREPARING A CASE AND NEGOTIATING RESULTS

At the beginning of a case, I must assume that my client and I are preparing for a trial. My staff and I prepare for court by obtaining and reviewing all of the available information. We analyze police reports, accident reports, questionnaires that help our clients share all that they remember about their particular situations, breath and blood test results from the Department of Forensic Science, and videos if available. I examine all of this information to look for every possible legal, factual, medical, or scientific defense. I then discuss the strengths and weaknesses of the case and the possible defenses with my clients. Being prepared for trial places us in the best position to point out any weaknesses in the prosecution's case or to take advantage of any problems the prosecution may face on the day of court. Sometimes discussing these issues with the prosecutor generates favorable offers that avoid the uncertainties of trial.

Certain DUI charges are more likely to generate plea agreements than others. One example of this is a case in which a client is accused of a second or subsequent DUI and the prior DUI occurred in another state. The Virginia Code provides that in order for a person to be found guilty of a subsequent offense based on an out-of-state prior conviction, the law of the other state must be substantially similar to Virginia's law for the particular charge. It can be challenging for the prosecution to prove the validity of the out-of-state order and that the law in effect at the time of the out-of-state conviction is substantially similar to Virginia's law. It is sometimes possible, therefore, for the client to plead guilty to a lesser offense, such as a first DUI instead of a second DUI.

Additionally, DUI cases which involve accidents are often resolved by agreements. The prosecution must prove certain additional elements in accident cases in order to introduce the defendant's BAC. These factors include showing that the defendant did not have access to alcohol after the accident and that he was arrested within three hours of the accident. The prosecution also has an additional burden when the defendant's BAC is determined by a blood test instead of a breath test. In order to introduce a blood test result in court, the prosecution must have the person who drew the blood and the person who analyzed the blood sample appear before the judge. The complications of proof and obtaining the necessary witnesses can sometimes result in negotiated results in accident cases that are beneficial to clients.

WHAT ARE THE PENALTIES FOR A DUI CONVICTION IN VIRGINIA?

Virginia Code Section 18.2-270 provides mandatory minimum sentencing requirements for people who are convicted of DUI and imposes enhanced penalties for cases that involve a high BAC and/or a subsequent offense. A judge must sentence someone who is convicted of a first offense DUI whose BAC is below 0.15 as follows: fine between $250 and $2,500, one year license suspension, completion of the Virginia Alcohol Safety Action Program (VASAP), and installation of an ignition interlock system for 6–12 months. Although there is no mandatory jail sentence for a first offense DUI with a BAC under 0.15, judges typically order a suspended jail sentence that could be imposed if the person fails to complete VASAP or does not remain of good behavior. In most cases, a first offender does not go to jail other than at the time of the arrest, receives a restricted license to drive for work, school, and certain other defined purposes on the day of court, and receives a fine close to the $250 minimum.

With respect to the alcohol level, even for a first offense, jail will be imposed for a BAC of 0.15 or above. In Virginia, a BAC of 0.15 to 0.20 will result in a five-day mandatory minimum jail sentence and if the BAC is above 0.20 the jail sentence will increase to a mandatory minimum of 10 days.

The penalties for a DUI conviction increase dramatically for a second offense. The judge must order the defendant's license to be suspended for three years and the minimum fine increases to $500. If the second offense occurs within five years of the first offense, there is a mandatory minimum 20-day jail sentence and the defendant will not be eligible to apply for a restricted license until one year after the date of the conviction. If the second offense occurs within five to ten years of the first offense, then the mandatory minimum jail sentence is ten days and a restricted license may be obtained after four months. In both cases the judge may impose the ignition interlock machine for as long as the person has a restricted license.

The BAC is a significant factor in a second offense. The mandatory minimum jail sentence for a high BAC doubles when attached to a second offense. Thus, a person who is convicted of a second offense DUI with an elevated BAC will receive 10 mandatory days of jail with a BAC of 0.15 to 0.20 or a minimum of 20 days of jail if the BAC is over 0.20. Significantly, the mandatory jail for a high BAC is in addition to the mandatory jail for the second offense itself. This means that if a person is convicted of a second offense DUI within five years of a first offense and has a BAC over 0.20, then he would receive a mandatory minimum jail sentence of 20 days for the second offense, plus at least 20 days of jail for the high BAC, for a total of at least 40 days in jail.

A third offense DUI conviction is a Class 6 felony. This means the loss of certain rights (such as voting, serving as a notary, and possessing a firearm) in addition to the penalties imposed by the court. Being found guilty of a third DUI results in an indefinite license suspension and no opportunity to apply for a restricted license until three years after the conviction. The minimum fine for a third DUI is $1,000. The sentencing range for a third DUI conviction is one to five years with a mandatory minimum time in jail of six months for a third offense within five years and at least three months in jail if the third offense is within five to ten years of the priors.

In addition to the mandatory sentencing requirements of the Virginia Code, judges evaluate several other factors to determine whether a DUI sentence should include enhanced penalties. These factors include: blood alcohol level, refusal to submit to blood alcohol testing, whether or not the driver caused an accident, degree of cooperation with law enforcement, any additional charges against the defendant, and any prior criminal history. Moreover, many judges consider personal injuries to others as an aggravating factor that justifies imposing or increasing time in jail. In one of my first offense DUI cases, the driver injured his passenger and received a six-month jail sentence (three months to serve after good time credit) and in another first-offense DUI case the driver injured a couple who was driving another vehicle and received a twelve-month jail sentence, which he appealed to the next level court. Although most first offense DUI cases do not involve any active jail time, the extent of the injuries in these two cases provoked the judges to deal more harshly with the defendants.

It is important to note that judges consider lack of cooperation with the police when they make their sentencing determinations. Two reckless driving cases that I handled demonstrate how judges react adversely to conflict between the client and the police. The two clients were in similar situations with comparable speeds and the same judge. The first driver saw his charge amended from the misdemeanor of reckless driving to a traffic infraction. However, the second driver was found guilty of reckless driving. The driver who was convicted of reckless driving had ranted and cursed at the police officer. The judge was simply unwilling to give that driver a break after he had been so discourteous and uncooperative with the officer.

One situation that sometimes affects sentencing is a client's past criminal history. If a client had a DUI conviction more than ten years before the new charge, then the prior offense cannot be used to elevate the new charge to a second offense. However, the prosecutor or the judge may argue that the person should not be treated the same as someone who is truly a first offender. This argument is sometimes successful in obtaining a more severe sentence than would be typical for someone without the prior record.

How Should I Plead At Court?

When my client and I appear in court, the judge will ask us how we plead. We have three options. My client can plead guilty, not guilty, or no contest. Each plea communicates something different to the judge and to the prosecutor.

By pleading guilty, my client declares that he is responsible for the offense he is charged with. Sometimes a guilty plea to one charge is part of an agreement for the dismissal or amendment of other charges. At other times, a guilty plea may be the result of negotiations for a concession on sentencing. There are also situations where the strength of the prosecution's case is so great that entering a guilty plea before the judge may help to avoid a more severe sentence.

A no contest plea indicates that we believe that the prosecution's evidence is sufficient for a judge to find my client guilty. We may take issue with certain parts of the prosecution's case but conclude that we are unlikely to prevail at trial. The no contest plea allows my client to avoid pleading guilty while also having an opportunity to explain the circumstances or other mitigating factors to the judge.

A plea of not guilty requires the prosecution to prove the case against my client. Pleading not guilty does not necessarily mean that we are pleading innocent. We may not dispute the fact that my client committed the act he is charged with, but a not guilty plea places the burden of proof on the prosecution. The prosecutor must prove each element of the offense that the defendant is charged with. In a DUI case, the prosecutor must prove that the police had a reasonable suspicion that justified stopping the defendant, that they had probable cause for arresting the defendant, and that the evidence as a whole demonstrates guilt beyond a reasonable doubt.

My responsibility as a defense lawyer is to obtain the best possible outcome for people who have been charged with criminal and traffic offenses. Since my work lies on the defense side, my goal is to present my clients and their cases in a manner that will result in the court erring on the side of mercy. The famous William Blackstone stated in his *Commentaries on the Laws of England* that, "... it is better that ten guilty persons escape, than that one innocent suffer,"[1] while Benjamin Franklin went as far as commenting in a letter he wrote in 1785 that "… it is better 100 guilty Persons should escape than that one innocent Person should suffer."[2]

Based on that time-honored reasoning, I believe that everyone deserves a fighting chance to plead his case and have his day in court. Although there are times when I believe that a trial will not be in my client's best interest, the client is the final decision maker about whether to present the case to the judge at a trial or as an agreement with the prosecution. I counsel my clients about the relative strengths and weaknesses of both sides of the case and the possible outcomes at trial and then permit them to decide how to proceed.

Sometimes clients choose to pursue a trial even when it is the riskier option for their case. For some, the idea of accepting an offer from a prosecutor would be worse than losing at trial. One morning, I handled DUI cases for two men who were both facing several other charges in addition to their DUIs, such as open container, refusal, and reckless driving. In each case, I was able to negotiate with the prosecutor that, in exchange for a guilty plea to the DUI, the prosecutor would dismiss all of the other charges. This was a generous offer based on the facts of these two cases. The first client liked the idea of ending up with only one conviction and avoiding the consequences of the other charges. He also appreciated the fact that the agreement would assure him of the minimum sentence for the DUI. The second client decided that he wanted to go to trial because he wished to tell the judge his side of what happened. He was convicted of every single charge. We appealed and eventually negotiated a better result, but he had to incur the additional time and costs involved in the appeal process. However, he was glad with the outcome because he placed greater value on "having a fighting chance" and "going down swinging." For him, the trial was preferable because he had gotten his day in court.

HOW CAN YOU REPRESENT SOMEONE WHO IS GUILTY?

Most of the people who contact me are first offenders and the majority of their cases involve blood alcohol contents that are not at enhanced levels. DUI is not a crime that requires a criminal intent. It simply involves operating a motor vehicle with a BAC of 0.08 or more or while under the influence of alcohol, drugs, or a combination of alcohol and drugs. This means that anyone who consumes alcohol or prescription drugs could potentially be arrested for DUI if operating a motor vehicle. The nature of alcohol is that it causes people to underestimate their level of intoxication or overestimate their ability to drive. The reality that it could happen to anyone is seen in the fact that I have represented people from all walks of life, including police officers, nurses, teachers, business owners, college students, and military personnel. I believe that each person has a right to defend his case and to challenge the prosecution's evidence.

In addition to the individual's desire to have his day in court, trials offer a social benefit. Whether or not a person is guilty, the trial scenario is a means of accountability for the police and the prosecution. The trial process reveals whether or not suspects are appropriately stopped and arrested and provides a means of protecting people's Fourth Amendment rights.

A challenging situation arises when someone is either innocent or the circumstances generate a great deal of sympathy for the client. This type of case can be more stressful because it brings an additional element to the desire to obtain the best result for the client. In one particular instance, my client was a college student who was charged with DUI when she fell asleep in her car with the engine running. Virginia's DUI law does not require that the vehicle be in motion. Instead, "operating a motor vehicle" includes simply placing the key in the ignition. My client started her car for heat and then took a nap. Although she never moved the vehicle, she was charged with operating a vehicle under the influence of alcohol. This was a disturbing case because my client was not moving her car and had not placed anyone in harm's way. Nevertheless, she was charged with DUI just like someone who was caught weaving or crossing lane lines. I felt that she deserved a vigorous defense to try to avoid the DUI. Although my client was found guilty in the first trial, we were able to obtain a lesser charge on appeal to the next level court.

I believe that attorneys need to offer a proper defense for someone, even if that person is clearly guilty, because the system cannot pick and choose who is worthy of being represented. We must have a fair system so that everyone who wants to mount a defense is able to present that defense and have an opportunity to let a judge decide the case. I further believe that a fair legal system protects both individual defendants and our society by providing accountability in arrest and prosecution decisions.

REASONABLE SUSPICION VS PROBABLE CAUSE

Before a police officer stops a driver, he must have a reasonable suspicion that a crime or traffic violation is occurring. In 1994, the Virginia Court of Appeals explained that "in order to justify an investigatory stop of a vehicle, the officer must have some reasonable, articulable suspicion that the vehicle or its occupants are involved in, or have recently been involved in, some form of criminal activity."[3]

This low threshold permits the police to stop vehicles with little evidence of misconduct. The appellate courts have determined that many slight infractions and unusual circumstances are satisfactory pretexts for a stop. For example, courts have concluded that the police had reasonable suspicion to justify a stop for such varied reasons as unlit taillights, a license plate letter not being visible, passengers throwing objects out of the car window, and drivers matching the description of vehicle owners whose licenses were suspended. In Virginia, even when the officer's intent is to search for drugs or some other criminal activity that is not readily observable, any slight infraction may justify the stop. The officer's motive in stopping the vehicle does not matter as long as he can find some basis for explaining that he had "more than a hunch" that a traffic or criminal violation was occurring.

Probable cause refers to the arrest decision, as compared to the basis for the stop itself. For probable cause, which is a higher threshold than reasonable suspicion, the officer looks at the totality of the circumstances to decide whether "the facts and circumstances within the arresting officer's knowledge and of which he has reasonably trustworthy information are sufficient in themselves to warrant a man of reasonable caution in the belief that an offense had been or is being committed."[4] The police officer considering an arrest evaluates the driving behavior, the driver's personal appearance, the ability to perform field sobriety tests, and the result of a preliminary breath test if one is taken.

CONTACT WITH THE POLICE

Whenever a police officer approaches a vehicle, he will be alert to determine whether the driver exhibits signs of being under the influence of alcohol or drugs. He may have stopped the driver due to simple speeding or a broken taillight, but upon speaking with the driver he will also be looking for clues regarding other possible offenses. As he approaches the vehicle, the officer will be wondering, "Does this person have slurred speech?" or "Does this person have an odor of an alcoholic beverage?" The officer will look at the driver's eyes to determine if they are bloodshot or watery and listen to the person's speech to determine if it is slow or slurred. He will also listen for admissions, such as acknowledgement of drinking or of having been to a club or bar. He will observe any difficulties the driver may have in locating and presenting a driver's license or vehicle registration. These are just a few of the clues or indicators that the police are trained to look for in evaluating whether further investigation is required.

In addition to the foregoing examples, the National Highway Traffic Safety Administration (NHTSA) has also noted the following indicators that someone may be under the influence of alcohol: difficulty exiting the vehicle, slow responses to the officer's questions, asking the officer to repeat questions, leaning on objects for balance, and difficulty standing or walking without losing balance. Other factors that will cause the police to be suspicious are the presence of alcohol in the vehicle and any attempt to mask the odor of alcohol, such as mouthwash, perfume, or lighting a cigarette[5].

FIELD SOBRIETY TESTS

When the police suspect that the driver is under the influence of alcohol or drugs they usually offer the driver the opportunity to complete a series of tests. The rationale for the tests is that they help the police determine whether or not to make an arrest. Actually, since the tests are inherently difficult to perform, they generally serve as a way for the police to bolster their case instead of as a means for people who are not under the influence to prove they should be released.

The two types of field sobriety tests are pre-exit tests and standardized field sobriety tests (SFSTs).

The pre-exit tests include all of the non-standardized tests that police use to evaluate whether to pursue a DUI investigation. Several of them may be conducted while the driver remains in his vehicle, such as reciting the alphabet, counting backwards, and counting one's fingers. Others require the driver to exit the vehicle, such as touching finger to nose. Some police officers use unusual tests, such as having the suspect drop a coin and pick it up or simply watching the subject stand with his eyes closed to determine whether he sways. However, none of these non-standardized tests has been found to assist in estimating a person's blood alcohol level.

The National Highway Traffic Safety Administration (NHTSA) conducted a series of studies[6] to determine the accuracy of field sobriety tests. One of the goals was to find tests that would help the police determine whether the driver they were investigating had a blood alcohol level of 0.10 or higher. They did not design the tests as a means of determining degree of impairment. Only three of the tests were identified as having a fair degree of accuracy in determining whether or not a driver had a blood alcohol level above 0.10. Those three tests are the One-Leg-Stand Test, the Walk-and-Turn Test (sometimes called the Nine-Step Walk-and-Turn), and the Horizontal Gaze Nystagmus Test.[7]

The first test, the One Leg Stand, requires the driver to stand on one foot while counting out loud. The driver chooses which foot he wants to stand on. The officer then instructs the driver to place his hands at his sides, raise the other foot six inches from the ground, look at that foot, and count aloud. The officer may instruct the subject to count to a certain number or he may tell the person to remain in that position until told to set his foot down. Either way, the standardized test requires the person to hold his foot up for 30 seconds. During the test, the officer watches for four possible clues: swaying while balancing, using arms to balance, hopping, or putting the foot down too early. If the person exhibits any two of the four clues, he fails the test. The studies show that if someone fails the One-Leg-Stand Test there is a 65% chance that the person's blood alcohol level is above 0.10.

The second test, the Walk-and-Turn or Nine-Step Walk-and-Turn, begins with the driver being placed in an instruction stance. The officer instructs the driver to stand with one foot in front of the other with the heel of one foot touching the heel of the other foot. The driver has to stand in that position without moving while the officer gives further instructions. The driver is then told to take nine steps, touching heel to toe, while counting each step out loud and keeping hands at the sides. After completing the first nine steps, the driver must complete a turn and then walk nine steps back to the beginning. The officer looks for eight possible clues during this test. The person fails the test if he exhibits any two of the eight clues: trouble maintaining balance in the instruction stance, starting the test too soon, stopping while walking, missing heel to toe, stepping off-line, using arms for balance, having a problem with the turn, and taking the wrong number of steps. The NHTSA research shows that a failure to properly complete the Walk-and-Turn Test indicates there is a 68% chance that the person's blood alcohol level is above 0.10.

The third test is the Horizontal Gaze Nystagmus (HGN). Nystagmus is an involuntary jerking of the eye that occurs after someone consumes alcohol. During the test, the person must stand still and follow a stimulus with his eyes. The stimulus could be the officer's finger, a flashlight, or a pen. The officer observes whether the subject can follow the stimulus with his eyes while also following instructions, such as not turning his head.

The clues for the HGN test are as follows: lack of smooth pursuit as the eyes follow the stimulus, nystagmus occurring at maximum deviation, and nystagmus occurring before 45 degrees. "Smooth pursuit" refers to the ability to follow the stimulus. "Nystagmus at maximum deviation" means that the involuntary jerking of the eye is observed when the eye is turned completely to the right or left. "Nystagmus before 45 degrees" indicates that the eye is jerking before it reaches a 45-degree angle as it turns from looking forward to the side while following the stimulus. Since each of the three clues can be observed in each eye, there are a total of six possible clues. If someone displays four of the six clues then there is a 77% chance that the person's blood alcohol level is above 0.10 percent.[8]

The HGN Test is not accepted by all judges. One reason for controversy regarding the HGN Test is that its accuracy was evaluated in a clinical setting and not in actual road test conditions. In a clinical setting, it was considered the most accurate of the SFSTs. However, few police are medically trained and the roadside is not an ideal testing location. Another aspect of skepticism about the test is that many factors can cause nystagmus other than alcohol. Nystagmus could result from the motion or lights of passing cars, emergency lights, or changing traffic signals in the subject's line of vision while being tested. Additionally, substances other than alcohol, such as aspirin, can cause nystagmus. Furthermore, prior concussions have been known to provoke a nystagmus reaction and some people naturally have a degree of nystagmus in their eyes.

SHOULD I TAKE THE FIELD SOBRIETY TESTS?

The field sobriety tests are voluntary in Virginia. No legal requirement exists for a person to participate in any of the roadside tests. Drivers have the absolute right to decline the One-Leg-Stand Test, the Walk-and-Turn Test, or any of the other field sobriety tests. The caveat is that, although the field tests can be refused, the prosecutor is entitled to comment on refusal to take the field tests as evidence of attempting to conceal guilt.

This does not mean that taking the field sobriety tests is in your best interest. These tests are used to help the police decide whether or not to arrest a suspect for DUI. I believe that people should decline the field sobriety tests. Even the standardized field sobriety tests which NHTSA found to be most accurate are wrong almost one-third of the time. This means that one-third of the results are false positives or false negatives. A case without any field sobriety test results limits the evidence against the defendant. For example, if a person is stopped for speeding and refuses all of the field tests and then either refuses the breath test or has a low BAC, the only evidence of DUI would be the officer's observations of the person's appearance.

I once spoke at a seminar for a paralegal association and had a participant try the Walk-and-Turn Test. The results were so poor that the participant would have failed the test and been arrested on suspicion of DUI. The paralegals asked me, "What would have happened if he wasn't drinking and then he was arrested because his field test was so bad?" I replied, "Once he blew into the preliminary breath test device and it did not show the presence of alcohol, the police would have suspected drugs. He would have been arrested and taken to a hospital for a blood draw to determine which drugs were in his system. He would have been charged with DUI and a trial date would have been set since they would not have known the blood result right away. Until the blood test results were received, the prosecution would have assumed that the defendant was under the influence of drugs instead of being fatigued, suffering from a medical condition, or simply having poor balance." It was a good demonstration of the unreliability of this type of testing.

On the other hand, I recommend that a person take the preliminary breath test (PBT), a handheld breath test device offered at the scene of the arrest. Normally, the PBT results are not disclosed to the judge in a DUI trial. They are not considered accurate enough to be introduced as evidence. Nevertheless, a low BAC on this test can result in the driver avoiding a DUI charge.

Additionally, it is important to understand that by driving on the roads of Virginia, drivers are consenting to submit to a breath or blood test to determine whether they are under the influence of alcohol or drugs. Refusing to submit to BAC testing at a police station, jail, or hospital will result in a separate charge of refusal. For a first offense, refusal is considered a civil penalty, but the consequence of being found guilty is suspension of the driver's license for one year.

CONCLUSION

I want people to understand that a DUI charge should not be taken lightly. Once charged with DUI, it is important to find an attorney who is experienced in dealing with these cases, not just a general practitioner. Lawyers who participate in the National College for DUI Defense (NCDD) and other bar associations which focus on DUI defense receive training that helps them improve their ability to represent people charged with this offense. Through such associations, they are better able to remain current on best practices for DUI defense and to obtain advice from fellow DUI practitioners. Moreover, some defenses are unique to DUI charges, so it is imperative that a lawyer be familiar with all of the "ins and outs" of DUI defense.

People need to acknowledge that they risk arrest if they drink any quantity of alcohol and drive a vehicle. Without taking an actual measurement with a preliminary breath testing device, people are only guessing their BAC when they drive. In fact, even if someone knew his exact BAC at the time he entered his vehicle, he would not know whether his BAC was rising or falling or what the BAC would be at the time of being stopped or taking a breath test. In fact, one of the defenses that attorneys use in a DUI case is the argument that a person's BAC may have risen between the time of driving and the time it is measured. When a person consumes a large amount of alcohol a short time before driving, his BAC will remain low for a period of time until the alcohol is fully absorbed. It is possible that even though a person was at a 0.06 BAC when entering his car, his BAC could rise to 0.08 or higher by the time he is stopped and taken for a breath test. Many people tell me, "I didn't think I was under the influence," or, "I wasn't feeling the effects." The uncertainty of BAC measurement makes it too risky to drive at all after consuming any amount of alcohol. Calling for a taxicab is similar to an insurance premium, paying a small amount to avoid a very expensive and potentially traumatic alternative.

One of my former clients, a college student, serves as a good example of the risk of driving after drinking. He did everything right throughout the first part of the evening. He took a cab when he went out with friends to the clubs and then walked between the clubs. They even took a cab ride home. However, after they returned home they decided that they were hungry and my client drove everyone to head out for something to eat. My client thought that enough time had passed since his last drink. Unfortunately, he made the wrong decision. Drinking and driving is *not* a risk worth taking.

(This content should be used for informational purposes only. It does not create an attorney-client relationship with any reader and should not be construed as legal advice. If you need legal advice, please contact an attorney in your community who can assess the specifics of your situation.)

References:

[1]"Sir William Blackstone" *Commentaries on the Laws of England*, 9th ed., book 4, chapter 27, p. 358, (1783, reprinted 1978).

[2]*The Writings of Benjamin Franklin*, ed. Albert H. Smyth, vol. 9, p. 293 (1906).

[3]Logan v. Commonwealth, 452 S.E.2d 364, 19 Va. App. 437 (Va. App., 1994), citing Murphy v. Commonwealth, 9 Va. App. 139, 143-44, 384 S.E.2d 125, 127 (1989).

[4]Saunders v. Commonwealth, 218 Va. 294, 237 S.E.2d 150, 155 (1977), citing Draper v. United States, 358 U.S. 307, 313, 79 S. Ct. 329, 3 L.Ed.2d 327 (1959); Schaum v. Commonwealth, 215 Va. 498, 500, 211 S.E.2d 73, 75 (1975).

[5]*DWI Detection and Standardized Field Sobriety Testing—Student Manual,* February 2006 Edition: U.S. Department of Transportation, Chapter VI.

[6]http://www.nhtsa.gov/people/injury/alcohol/sfst/introduction.htm

[7]*DWI Detection and Standardized Field Sobriety Testing—Student Manual,* February 2006 Edition: U.S. Department of Transportation, Chapter VII.

[8]http://www.nhtsa.gov/people/injury/enforce/nystagmus/hgntxt.html

8

NORTH CAROLINA: A DWI OVERVIEW

by Matthew J. Golden, Esq.

Matthew J. Golden, Esq.

Matthew J. Golden, Attorney at Law, PLLC
Raleigh, North Carolina
www.mjgoldenlaw.com

Matthew attended the University of Richmond for his Undergraduate degree and Campbell University School of Law for his Juris Doctor. Matthew has courtroom experience trying DWI cases from both the prosecution side and the defense side.

Since starting his own law practice over 3 years ago, Matthew has been recognized by his peers as an aggressive, knowledge-able attorney who fights hard for his clients. Matthew has zealously defended DWI clients in front of both judges and juries in Wake County, NC.

The online leading legal service marketer, Avvo, awarded Matthew its Client's Choice awards in 2013 and 2014 for the areas of DWI Defense and Criminal Defense. Matthew enjoys spending his free time with his wife Lauren, and their dog Rex, at their home in Raleigh, NC.

NORTH CAROLINA: A DWI OVERVIEW

Each state has different laws regarding driving while impaired (DWI) and driving under the influence (DUI). For example, New York has DUI laws while North Carolina only has laws making DWI an illegal act. In a North Carolina DWI case, the State must prove that the person was operating a motor vehicle while impaired by alcohol or drugs. The definition of a motor vehicle is generally something that is propelled or motorized by the power of a person. Therefore, you cannot be guilty of DWI while riding a horse, but you can be found guilty of DWI on a tractor, golf cart, and even a bicycle.

Oddly enough, a bicycle does fall under the category of a motor vehicle for the purposes of DWI, because a bicycle is classified as "mechanical" by law. A bike-related DWI is therefore classified as the same offense as a car-related DWI, which seems ridiculous. I think that the law should address DWI charges on bicycles differently than it addresses DWIs in other vehicles. The strangest case that I've ever heard involved someone here in North Carolina's Wake County, who was charged with DWI on a motorized cooler. The cooler had beer and ice in it like a regular cooler, but also had a little engine at the bottom. The person was scooting around on the cooler at a tailgate gathering, and he received a DWI because the cooler was characterized as a "motor vehicle."

The State must also prove that the person operated the motor vehicle on a highway, street, or public vehicular area within the state. That definition includes public roads, highways, public parking lots, and normal traffic areas. The definition does not include any private driveway, because it is not a public vehicular area. In a private driveway, even if the officer has proof that you operated a vehicle while impaired, that is insufficient evidence for a DWI charge. Alternatively, if the officer observes you driving on a public road and then you pull into a private driveway, you can still be charged with a DWI.

Finally, the State must prove that the person was driving while under the influence of an impairing substance. Impairment can be measured with a blood or breath test. If your blood alcohol concentration is measured via either a blood or breath test at 0.08 or higher, the State can prove impairment. North Carolina's law also states that any amount of a Schedule One controlled substance in your system is per se impairment. Alternatively, if you do not show a blood alcohol level of 0.08 or higher, you can still be classified as "appreciably impaired." This term means that the driver's physical and mental faculties were noticeably impaired due to the presence of an impairing substance.

For example, if someone takes an Ambien and then drives, that person can be charged with a DWI based on the decision to drive after taking a Schedule I prescribed medicine that is known to affect one's physical and/or mental faculties. If that same person registered a 0.08 or higher on the Intox EC/IR II breath test, he or she could be charged under the "0.08 prong" as well. Finally, if that person refused to take a breath test, and a blood test was not available, yet the officer concluded the person was impaired based on poor performance of field sobriety tests and other observations, he or she could be charged under the "appreciable impairment" prong. When operating a vehicle, it's important to know what is in your system and what you can and cannot do with that substance in your system. Typically, there are warning labels on bottles of medication clearly stating that a person should not operate machinery or vehicles while taking the medication.

WHEN CAN AN OFFICER PULL YOU OVER FOR DWI?

Before an officer can pull you over for a suspected DWI, he must have a reasonable suspicion that leads up to the stop. The courts define "reasonable suspicion" as more than a hunch that some type of criminal activity is in progress. For example, speeding or driving too slow is against the law, and the officer can legally stop you for either of those activities. Any Chapter 20 traffic violation observed by law enforcement is enough of a reason to initiate a stop. Signs of impaired driving, such as *continuous* swerving or unusual driving activity, can also be valid for a stop, even if it doesn't arise to a per se traffic violation. If a stop is not valid, dismissal of all evidence is warranted, even if the defendant turns out to be highly intoxicated. Therefore, when attorneys defend a DWI, we focus heavily on reasonable suspicion.

The ability to gather a vast amount of information is probably the most important tool that a DWI attorney can use to defend his client. More information gives an attorney a better chance to discover an issue that might help in preparing a defense.

Dash-cam videos are now a huge part of the discovery process and are very informative in the creation of a defense.

When an officer stops a driver, the dash-cam video typically records the entire stop from a few moments before the blue lights are activated, through the field sobriety tests and the arrest. Attorneys should subpoena the video to determine if there is a question to whether or not the officer had reasonable suspicion to make the stop and consequently observe the driver's performance on sobriety tests. Many times, I've had clients who either thought they had aced or failed the tests; later, the video tells both of us a quite different story. Many recent cases have defined what constitutes reasonable suspicion to make a stop. These cases have been focused on the car weaving plus another factor: speeding, time of night, proximity to bars or restaurants, proximity to alcohol-selling establishments, a blank stare on the driver's face, or a look of confusion. The best types of cases to challenge on reasonable suspicion is those in which the video shows good driving for an extended period of time where there is only one or two instances of weaving. Continuous weaving, coupled with a late time of day, has been found to be enough for reasonable suspicion here in NC.

Therefore, if you are within your lane but you swerve once or twice, this is probably not enough to pull you over without another factor. There is a "failure to maintain lane control" infraction in NC that may allow the officer to pull you over if the judge finds a substantive violation. Unfortunately, it has become more difficult to contest "reasonable suspicion" because judges want the case to proceed to see what happened after the stop. Most often, the courts have taken the position of deferring to the officer's judgment when it comes to deciding if there was reasonable suspicion to make the traffic stop. While the burden of proof for the State is very low to prove reasonable suspicion, an invalid stop can lead to a dismissal of a DWI in which there is overwhelming evidence of impairment.

WHAT HAPPENS DURING A DWI STOP?

Clients often ask me—after they have been charged, unfortunately—what should I have done differently in my interactions with the law enforcement officer? Generally speaking, the less information you provide to the officer, the less evidence of impairment they can obtain to use against you in court. Of course, do not disobey the request or instruction of an officer. However, this is my best advice for a person who gets pulled over: be polite, be cooperative, but do not answer any questions. Politely tell the officer that you would rather not answer that question. That advice also extends to field sobriety tests. Many people think, "Well, I've only had a beer or two. I'll get out. I can do this test. No problem." They do not realize that standardized field sobriety tests are extremely hard to pass, even if you are dead sober. In a controlled experiment, I directed someone (who had not imbibed any alcohol) to take the Walk-and-Turn test and the One-Leg-Stand test—two of the standardized field sobriety tests. On the Walk-and-Turn test, he showed eight clues. On the One-Leg-Stand test, he showed four clues. You must be coordinated, have good balance, and be in shape to actually perform and pass those tests to an officer's satisfaction.

Another test is the portable breath test (PBT), often given on the side of the road to assist the officer in forming probable cause for arrest. An officer will say, "Okay. Blow into this for me." The officer does not say this as if you have an option to decline. However, in North Carolina, there is no penalty for refusing to take a portable breath test on the side of the road. You are not required to take a PBT at the scene, which is different from the actual chemical breath analysis test at the police station or the detention center. The officer may become frustrated and even a bit angry because you are subverting his investigation. In reality, you are looking out for your best interests by limiting the evidence that can be used against you. At the first point of contact, the officer is trying to trip you up. He is trying to get as many clues and observations as possible to include in his report in order to build a case against you. The clues may include red or glassy eyes, an odor of alcohol, slurred speech, difficulty following instructions, or difficulty in retrieving your license. Let's say that you just do not know the location of your registration, because you have not gotten it out in 6 months or a year, and you cannot find it. The officer will say, "Oh, he couldn't find his registration. That's a sign of impairment."

The officer is gathering sufficient evidence to present probable cause to a magistrate judge that you were driving while impaired. At this point in the stop, because he's gathering further evidence, the officer does not have to prove "beyond reasonable doubt" but only "more likely than not" that you were driving while impaired. Be very careful about everything that you do or say from the moment of the stop. This includes making eye contact with the officer. The officer might say, "He didn't make eye contact," or "His windows were open on a chilly night when I pulled him over." Some of the clues noted by the officer might be part of a normal traffic encounter that has nothing to do with impairment, such as the inability to immediately retrieve a license, misplaced registration, or open windows for smoking. However, the officer will use any available clues to establish probable cause for a DWI arrest, without allowing for alternate reasons for those clues other than alcohol or drug-related impairment.

An officer making a stop will often ask these types of questions: "Did you drink alcohol? How much? What type? When was the last time you drank?" Think twice about answering any of those questions. Typically, after a few questions, the officer will ask you to step out of your car. At this point, you cannot refuse or disobey his instructions. If he demands that you step out of your car, do it, but don't use the door to balance. Do not lean on the hood when you have your hands on the hood. Avoid stumbling, tripping, or swaying; the officer will note these specific clues in his report. If you are asked to walk to the back or the front of the car, make sure that you walk straight and upright without swaying or leaning on the car. It is critical to keep your balance.

Typically, an officer relies heavily on the results of the standard-ized field sobriety tests. However, before administering those tests, some officers like to perform "pre-exit tests" before asking you to step out of the vehicle, such as counting backwards. The officer will make this task as difficult as possible by giving you numbers, such as 64 to 49 rather than 65 to 50. Another test might be saying your ABCs but the officer will ask you to say only a portion of the ABCs such as E through P. You must listen very carefully to the instructions, if you decide to do these tests, because performing the tests incorrectly will be just another clue for the officer. Another pre-exit test is the Finger Count test. The officer will ask you to touch your thumb to the tip of each finger of the same hand, while simultaneously counting from one to four, and then reversing the action and the counting. Remember that in North Carolina you can refuse these tests without incurring any penalties, and it is generally not in your best interest to do any of these non-standardized tests. To my knowledge, there are only three standardized tests recognized as valid in all 50 of our United States.

STANDARDIZED FIELD SOBRIETY TESTS

The National Highway Traffic Safety Administration (NHTSA) publishes the manual used to train officers to administer the three standardized field sobriety tests recognized by their organization. I own this manual and often use it during a trial. It is probably the most important single document that a DWI defense attorney can use in the defense of his client. When an officer is testifying about the tests that he administered, I can go right to the manual during cross-examination to pick apart his testimony and see if he administered the tests incorrectly or under inadequate conditions.

Horizontal Gaze Nystagmus (Hgn) Test

The first test is the Horizontal Gaze Nystagmus (HGN) test. During the HGN test, the officer is observing involuntary jerking of the eyes, which increases along with an increased amount of alcohol in the person's system. My biggest problem with the HGN test is that alcohol is not the sole cause of horizontal gaze nystagmus. In North Carolina, in order to correlate the HGN test with evidence of alcohol impairment, the officer administering the test must be qualified as an expert under the Daubert standard. The officer's testimony must be based upon sufficient facts or data, must be the product of reliable principles and methods, and the witness must have applied the principles and methods reliably to the facts of the case. It is always important to object if the officer has not yet been qualified as an HGN expert. I usually ask questions about the officer's background to challenge his credibility and qualifications for HGN test administration.

These are some of the questions that I ask: "Do you have any degrees in ophthalmology, optometry, or physiology? Have you ever taken any medical courses in eye physiology? Are you familiar with any other causes of HGN such as hypertension, caffeine, nicotine, or aspirin? What are the effects of these medical conditions on the muscles of the eye? Are you licensed to diagnose eye dysfunction? Did you receive specialized DWI impairment detection training, or just the basic law enforcement HGN training? How many hours have you spent in those courses, compared to the hours spent by other officers? Did physicians or optometrists teach these courses?" I then follow up with general questions such as, "What causes nystagmus? What causes jerking of the eye?"

Some officers are not familiar with the other types of nystagmus, such as rotational nystagmus that occurs after someone has been spun around or rotated rapidly, so that the inner ear fluid disturbs the eye movements. Caloric nystagmus occurs when there is fluid motion in the canals of the vestigial system; it's possible to test this condition by delivering warm water (or air) into one ear and cold water in the other. Optokinetic nystagmus occurs when the eyes fixate on objects that suddenly move out of sight, like strobe lights or rapidly moving lights. I have gotten the results of HGN tests excluded from the judge's consideration of evidence because the officer gave the test in front of his patrol car, where the flashing blue lights were rotating like strobe lights. Any one of these situations can result in nystagmus without the consumption of any alcohol. Medical problems or pathological disorders (brain tumors, brain damage, or diseases of the inner ear) can also cause nystagmus. All of these different types of nystagmus are discussed in the manual for the standardized field sobriety tests. Officers should be familiar with the types of nystagmus. If not, I object to the officer's qualification as an expert. Having said that, each state has different requirements for qualifying the officer before testimony or evidence from the HGN test can be admitted in court.

Problems arise when officers do not give proper directions on the HGN test or don't administer their part properly. The officer should say, "I'm going to check your eyes. Keep your head still and follow the stimulus (finger, pen, pencil, etc.) only with your eyes. Don't move your head. Keep following the stimulus with your eyes until I tell you to stop." Also, the stimulus should be 12 to 15 inches away from a suspect's nose and slightly above eye level. If the stimulus is not in the correct position, it is impossible for the officer to accurately estimate the 45-degree angle when checking for the onset of nystagmus prior to 45 degrees.

Another recurrent issue is the officer's failure to ask about medical conditions that could cause nystagmus or to check for equal-sized pupils and equal tracking. In most cases, if the person has equal-sized pupils and equal tracking, there is probably not a medical issue or medical impairment causing the eyes to move. If the suspect has a medical condition that could affect the test, the officer should not administer the test. Any person who voluntarily agrees to take the HGN test should tell the officer about any eye-related medical issues before starting the test.

The officer is looking for several clues when he administers the HGN test. The first clue is a lack of smooth pursuit. He checks each eye by moving the stimulus from the nose to the shoulder in about two seconds. This determines if the eye was able to follow the object smoothly or if there was a jerking motion. After this four-second test, if there was a lack of smooth pursuit, the officer should repeat that procedure. Prosecutors often ask this type of question at trial: "Did it appear as if the suspect's eyes were like windshield wipers on a dry windshield?" This analogy will give the district court judge a good visual image. In North Carolina, any DWI trial will take place in front of a judge (not a jury) unless the defendant appeals his DWI case to a superior court as a *trial de novo*, complete with new prosecutors and a jury.

The second clue is maximum deviation. The officer moves the object to the suspect's left side until the eye has gone as far as it can go and holds the object there for a minimum of four seconds. The officer is observing if the eye is jerking while it is stationary. Then the officer moves the object to the suspect's right side, holds it for four seconds and then repeats this test once more. The third part of the HGN test is moving the object towards the right, stopping near the shoulder's edge to check for nystagmus prior to reaching a 45-degree angle. This takes an additional four seconds. Again, the officer will move the object towards the right, stop near the shoulder, and wait for four seconds to see if there are any eye-jerking movements. If there are, the officer will repeat this part of the HGN test.

Walk-And-Turn Test

The Walk-and-Turn test is probably the most important indicator of impairment. Judges place high regard on the results of the Walk-and-Turn test. This test's location is very important. Often, attorneys find out that officers have pulled over the person on the side of the road, but the shoulder is slanted so the walking surface is not level or the road is still wet from rain. The NHTSA manual states that the surface must be dry, hard, level, and non-slippery. The surface is very important to the accuracy of the test. The dash-cam video definitely helps attorneys to see if the conditions during the test were correct.

Although the manual does not state that the officer cannot use an imaginary line, I believe that there should be a line in order for the test results to be valid. In many cases, officers say, "Okay, imagine a line and walk on it." My biggest gripe with this approach is that a designated straight line doesn't match with an imagined straight line. However, the officer must also consider the suspect's safety when performing the test. A person should not perform this test on a road or highway, in danger of other vehicular traffic, just so that the suspect is using a straight line painted on the roadway.

Another element of this test is the instruction phase. The officer should give the proper instructions according to the NHTSA manual in order for the test results to be valid. However, before beginning the test, the suspect should carefully listen and understand all of the instructions. To take the test, place your left foot on the line, your right foot in front of your left foot, place your arms down at your side, and remain in that position until the officer tells you to begin. Many people do not realize that the test begins with the officer giving the instructions. The officer will typically say, "When I tell you to start, take nine heel-to-toe steps. Turn and then take nine heel-toe steps back." The officer should also demonstrate the test by taking nine steps forward, turning, and taking nine steps back. During the instruction phase, the officer is watching for clues such as the suspect beginning the test before the officer completes the instructions or exhibiting any difficulty in understanding the instructions.

The officer should also give very specific instructions on the turn, which is not a normal turning activity. People often get marked down for doing an "improper turn" because the officer did not properly explain how to turn. This is the sequence: while keeping your front foot on the line, turn by taking a series of small steps until you are facing back down the line in the other direction, maintaining balance and your feet on the line. While you are walking, he should also tell you to "keep your arms at your side, watch your feet at all times, count your steps aloud, and don't stop walking until you finish." If the officer did not give the proper instructions, this will have a big impact on the results of the test. I make sure that the judge or the jury knows that the instructions were improper, which could be the reason for the suspect's poor performance on the test.

In evaluating the test performance, the officer is looking for at least eight clues from the suspect: stopping walking, missing heel-to-toe, stepping off the line, raising his arms, adding a few steps, starting before he was told to start, counting the steps, failing to make a proper turn, etc. On the defense side, attorneys should be looking for their own clues regarding officer conduct: standing at a safe distance, allowing or not allowing the defendant to resume the test after staggering, and relating proper or improper instructions.

Also, there are specific instructions on the evaluation of these clues and when an action can be counted as a clue. If the person stepped off the line, was his foot just barely or entirely off the line? There is a big difference between the person's foot not quite matching the center of the line and the person falling or stumbling six to twelve inches off of the line. If he missed heel-to-toe, did he miss heel-to-toe by more than half an inch? If not, that clue shouldn't be counted. Did he raise his arms more than six inches from the side? If he raised his arms by no more than six inches, that clue should not be counted.

One-Leg-Stand Test

The third and final standardized field sobriety test is the One-Leg-Stand test. It should also be done on a reasonably dry, hard, level, non-slip surface with adequate lighting. The officer should instruct the person, "Do not perform the test until I instruct you do so. Stand with your feet together and your arms at your side." (The officer should certainly demonstrate this part.) "When I tell you to start, raise one leg until your foot is approximately six inches off the ground, keeping your raised foot parallel to the ground. While holding the position, count aloud in the following manner: 1001, 1002, 1003, until you're told to stop." He should then demonstrate exactly what he wants the suspect to do before asking, "Do you understand the instructions?"

If you have any medical conditions such as knee surgeries or back problems, you must tell the officer before beginning the test. Understand that the One-Leg-Stand test is not easy to do even while sober; it is much more difficult to do with alcohol in your system. It is also much more difficult if you have a bad knee, back, or ankle.

The test should be stopped after 30 seconds. After 30 seconds, fatigue will set in, making it more likely that you will put your foot down due to fatigue rather than alcohol. In evaluating performance, an officer should check to see if the suspect put the foot down. If so, did the officer instruct the person to pick up his foot and continue counting from the point at which the foot touched the ground? Did the officer end the test or did he allow the person to continue? Did the officer remain still and observe from a safe distance?

Shoe height also affects a person's performance, both in the One-Leg-Stand and the Walk-and-Turn test. If you are wearing shoes with a heel of two inches or more, especially if you are a female wearing high heels, the officer should give you an opportunity to remove the shoes before beginning the test. The officer is looking for four clues: swaying, using the arms to balance, hopping, and putting the foot down.

WHAT HAPPENS IF YOU ARE TAKEN INTO CUSTODY?

If the officer believes that he has found probable cause, he will take the person to a detention center or police station to administer a breath test. As discussed above, in North Carolina, you have the right to refuse a breath test. However, think long and hard about whether or not to refuse a breath test. In North Carolina, there is an automatic 12-month license suspension for willful refusal. If it is not a willful refusal, you can challenge the suspension with a DMV hearing officer. For example, if you have asthma or another medical issue that prevents you from blowing into the device, you can offer the challenge that the refusal was not willful.

If you refuse the breath test, there is a very good chance that the officer will try to take your blood. Unless the suspect consents to a blood test, the officer must get a "blood search warrant" to draw blood. With a warrant, they can forcibly—and literally—strap you down and stick a needle into your arm to draw that blood, and there's not much that the suspect can do besides submit. Your blood sample will be sent to a lab for analysis, to determine the blood alcohol content (BAC), and your blood may also be tested for the presence of drugs. Currently in Wake County, NC, attorneys are seeing the results arrive within 30-60 days. If you willfully refuse the breath test, you will lose your license for a year, and the authorities will likely get your BAC anyway with a blood test. Even with a refusal suspension, you won't get any driving privileges back until six months after the beginning of the suspension.

If the officer decides not to take your blood or no nurse is available to take the blood, the State will not be able to determine the alcohol concentration in your blood. This does not mean that you will not be convicted of DWI. You can still be found guilty of being appreciably impaired by alcohol or another impairing substance. The State uses field sobriety tests as evidence to prove that you were appreciably impaired. If the State proves its case beyond a reasonable doubt, a judge or jury will look at the big picture that includes the field sobriety tests, your statements or admissions at the scene, possible alcohol-slurred speech, and your behavior at the scene. Even though the State might not have a breath test or blood test with a result of 0.08 or higher, it can still prove you are guilty of DWI. Furthermore, case law in North Carolina permits a judge to consider a refusal against you as a sign that you may have been impaired. It is risky to refuse a breath or blood test.

I'm often asked about case dismissals based on a lack of a Miranda warning. However, Miranda rules don't apply unless you are making statements after being placed in custody, which is typically when you're not free to terminate the encounter. If you're in custody, the officer hasn't asked any questions, and you're voluntarily blurting out voluntary statements like, "you got me, I had five drinks at the bar before you pulled me over," this will probably come in as evidence of an admission—even if the officer didn't advise you of your right to remain silent.

If you do choose to take a breath test, you can request the presence of a witness, who then has a certain amount of time to arrive at your location from the moment that you advise authorities of your request. In North Carolina, if the authorities start that test without waiting 30 minutes, you can file a motion to throw out the evidence, based on a few cases such as <u>State vs. Myers</u> 445 SE 2d 492 (N.C. App. 1995), and <u>State vs. Fergusion</u> 90 N.C. App 513 (1988). It's your right to have someone watch you take the test in order to present evidence to aid in your defense. If the State violates that right, a good attorney will file a pre-trial motion before a judge to quash the evidence.

THE TRIAL

If you decide to have a jury trial or your jurisdiction mandates one, the selection of jurors is a huge consideration. You want to have jurors who are sympathetic to your case, who will really think about the case in relation to the elements that the State must prove, rather than automatically assuming your guilt. It's also helpful if the jurors have had friends or family charged with a DWI—good people who simply made a bad decision on a particular night. Unfortunately, some jurors will see the defendant sitting in court and think to themselves, "Well, he must have done something wrong, or he wouldn't be sitting in court." Sometimes, as a defense attorney, it's good to have jurors who can use their emotions as well as their logic in making decisions.

The assistant district attorney in a DWI case generally looks for jurors who are very by-the-book and logicial, like engineers; the State doesn't want sympathetic jurors. The ADA will look for jurors who can set aside their emotions and look only at the elements of the crime and whether the State met each element of the crime to prove its case. When picking a jury, keep in mind the State's preferences as much as your preferences for the jurors' characteristics. As a defendant, you never want a juror who has had his or her life affected negatively by a DWI case. Maybe he or she was in an accident caused by an impaired driver or lost a loved one in a DWI accident. Attorneys ask those types of questions during jury selection to rule out those jurors.

Another recurring issue in DWI trials involves proof—whether or not the State can prove that the defendant was actually driving that motor vehicle. This arises in cases involving accidents. By the time that law enforcement officers arrive at the scene of the accident, the driver may not be found still behind the wheel of the car. However, case law in North Carolina suggests that if the keys are in the ignition and the engine is running, the driver is operating the motor vehicle, even though operation is technically defined as *control* of that vehicle. In this case, control is attributed to the person who placed the keys in the ignition. Often, an officer will ask the defendant if they were driving, and the defendant will truthfully say they were, making the State's case a little easier.

Sometimes, an admission by the defendant is not enough to meet the burden of proof. In the case of *State vs. Trexler* 316 N.C. 528, 533 (1986), the court stated that the State must have independent, corroborating evidence that the defendant was driving the vehicle to prove operation, even with an admission by the defendant. This is important in accident cases in which the driver left the scene and the officer later tracked down the driver. Corroborating evidence (independent of an admission) includes the car keys found in the defendant's pocket or a witness who saw the defendant running from the scene. If the defendant was standing near the vehicle at any point in time, and the engine was warm, that may be used a piece of corroborating evidence. Additionally, it's important to establish the relevant time period of driving in relation to the charge to meet this burden.

If an open container is found in the vehicle, this sometimes creates an issue. The person may have taken a few post-accident swigs to calm his nerves. If he admits this to the officer, the officer's job gets tougher in placing the driver behind the wheel at relevant time period after drinking. In a jury trial I had, the State had trouble proving that the driver was actually impaired while driving or that she had consumed alcohol before driving. She had crashed her car in an area within walking distance to several bars, became frustrated with the accident situation, and then visited a bar. Due to the frustration of damaging her vehicle, she consumed several shots of alcohol and several beers before returning to her car. An officer was present at the scene, and she found herself in handcuffs for DWI, even though the officer didn't know for sure whether or not she had consumed enough alcohol prior to driving the vehicle.

PENALTIES FOR DRIVING WHILE IMPAIRED

For a first-time offender in North Carolina, penalties are statute-based according to various levels. Level 5 is the most lenient level, while Level 1 is the most serious level for misdemeanor DWI charges. Level 5 generally applies to first offenses with court cost and fines between $600 and $800 and 24 hours of community service or 24 hours in jail. The judges usually give the defendant an option of community service or jail time. Depending on the level of the offense, other penalties include the requirement of a substance abuse assessment plus a treatment plan (minimum of 16 hours), higher insurance rates, extended jail time, higher fines, and loss of driving privileges. If the defendant has had a prior DWI conviction within the last seven years, he or she will spend a minimum of seven days in jail, unless that sentence is suspended for inpatient alcohol or drug treatment, or a continuous alcohol-monitoring device. Three or four prior DWI convictions may result in two years or more in prison. The penalties increase based on the date and severity of the previous convictions.

In North Carolina, an alcohol concentration of 0.15 or higher is an aggravating factor. You will not be able to get a limited driving privilege right away if that factor is proven beyond a reasonable doubt at sentencing. In district court, that means a judge. In superior court, a jury will determine aggravating or mitigating factor. If the 0.15 factor is proven, the defendant must wait 45 days after conviction, and then he or she will have to install an interlock device on the vehicle for one year. Afterward, he or she must provide proof to the judge of the device's installation. An interlock device is a essentially the "blow and go" device you hear about. Any driver of that vehicle cannot drive without blowing into this device before starting the car.

MITIGATING FACTORS THAT CAN REDUCE THE PENALTIES FOR DWI

I generally advise my clients to immediately get a substance abuse assessment. In NC, this is a mitigating factor for the judge to consider in deciding a penalty. Another mitigating factor is an alcohol concentration of 0.09 or lower. Other mitigating factors include a safe driving record within the previous five years, safe and lawful driving at the time leading up to the stop, and taking a lawfully prescribed drug for a medical condition, and the amount fell within your prescribed dose. Cooperation with the officer is another factor that judges will take into consideration. However, my best advice to clients is to politely decline to answer questions from the officer without an attorney present and to decline all field sobriety tests.

PRACTICAL TIPS TO AVOID DRINKING AND DRIVING

This is the single best way to avoid getting stopped for DWI: do not drink and drive. "How much can I can drink and drive?" is a very tough question because it really depends on an individual's metabolism, weight, and ability to tolerate alcohol. I shy away from saying, "If you only have one or two, you should be fine," because some people have two drinks and they are not fine. If you only have one drink, wait at least an hour before you drive.

DWI charges, when they involve a bench trial with a judge, can be very political. Judges in North Carolina are both appointed and elected. After their appointment, judges generally have to run for election to keep their seats, so they do not want to appear "soft" on DWIs for a very good reason. Keep that in mind when preparing a DWI defense. Judges are under a tremendous amount pressure from organizations like Mothers Against Drunk Driving because of the reality of so many DWI-related deaths in this country.

The National Transportation Safety Board has recommended that the legal blood alcohol limit be lowered from 0.08 to 0.05, which has already been adopted by over 100 countries worldwide. Obviously, this will meet strong opposition from many owners of restaurants and bars from fear of lower alcohol sales. In Raleigh, NC, where I practice, there is a newly created and federally funded DWI taskforce within Raleigh Police Department with four specific officers who do nothing but impaired driving enforcement. DWI arrests are on a tremendous rise in this state. Keep that in mind if you have had something to drink, and you are considering getting behind the wheel of a car.

Also, keep in mind that if you are going out for a drink, the best way to prevent a DWI is to designate a driver or flag a taxi. If you do drink and drive, keep in mind that the cards will be automatically stacked against you. If you are charged with DWI, it is important to hire a smart, aggressive attorney who will attack the issues in your case and is not afraid to challenge the State's evidence.

COST OF A DWI ATTORNEY

The cost will vary due to a number of factors: location, cost of living, severity of the offense, number of offenses, victim's injuries, or relation to a traffic accident. Hiring a good DWI attorney in Raleigh, North Carolina, will incur costs from $1,000 to $5,000, even for a misdemeanor DWI or a first offense. For example, if the DWI involves a serious injury or loss of life, the charges could be upgraded to manslaughter or murder, resulting in much higher attorney fees.

WHAT SHOULD I LOOK FOR IN A DWI ATTORNEY?

Find someone who knows the law, has experience in defending DWI cases, and makes you feel comfortable. Some of my friends ask me how I can represent a guilty person. I tell them that it is not an attorney's job to judge someone as guilty or not guilty. It is our job to defend the client vigorously, within the confines of ethics and law. It is the job to meet their burden of proof—guilty beyond a reasonable doubt. As defense attorneys, we are not doing our jobs if we don't hold the State responsible for meeting its burden of proof. Therefore, whether or not I think a person is guilty is ultimately not relevant to the way that

I handle the case. Some people come to the office and tell me flat out, "I'm guilty of this. I did this." That might be true, but the State is still required to prove its case.

If, for some reason, the officer did not follow proper procedure or you were denied access to a witness at a crucial time in the proceedings, your constitutional rights may have been violated. These types of errors by the State can have a huge impact on your case, even if it seems that the State has a rock solid case against you. I generally stay away from judging people on guilt and try my best to defend them with the facts at hand. Our job as DWI defense attorneys is to zealously fight for our client's rights and counsel them through this often difficult and stressful journey.

(This content should be used for informational purposes only. It does not create an attorney-client relationship with any reader and should not be construed as legal advice. If you need legal advice, please contact an attorney in your community who can assess the specifics of your situation.)

9

OFFICER DUI TRAINING:

MYTHS AND MISCONCEPTIONS OF IMPAIRED DRIVING INVESTIGATION

by James Minick, Esq.

James Minick, Esq.
Minick Law
Asheville, North Carolina
www.minicklaw.com

James Minick is the North Carolina DWI Guy and President of Minick Law, P.C. James decided DWI Defense would be a focal point of Minick Law's services and has assembled a team of DWI attorneys that are committed to remaining cutting edge on the constantly shifting landscape of DWI laws.

James concentrates his practice in DWI / DUI Defense and has handled hundreds of DWI cases throughout Western North

Carolina. The National Trial Lawyers Association has named him one of its Top 100 Trial Lawyers for 2014-2015. He is a General Member of the National College for DUI Defense. James has successfully completed the National Highway Traffic Safety Administration's course on DUI Detection and Standardized Field Sobriety Testing, a course taught to police officers to train them in DWI investigations.

OFFICER DUI TRAINING: MYTHS AND MISCONCEPTIONS OF IMPAIRED DRIVING INVESTIGATION

Police officers are, or at least should be, extensively trained before investigating and charging one of the most complex crimes in existence today: Driving While Impaired.[1] The National Highway Traffic Safety Administration (NHTSA)[2] has developed the curriculum that is commonly used to train officers in DUI Detection and Standardized Field Sobriety Testing (SFST). In its curriculum, NHTSA has outlined a list of clues or indicators of impairment that officers use to determine if a driver is impaired. NHTSA has also established field sobriety tests to be administered by the officer and has developed the guidelines for conducting those field sobriety tests. NHTSA outlines the DUI detection process—or as I like to call it, "the witch hunt"—in three phases.

PHASE ONE: VEHICLE IN MOTION

A. 24 Signs Of Impaired Driving

Officers are trained to look for twenty-four driving clues that are indicative of impaired drivers. For each of the 24 clues,[3]

NHTSA has developed a probability that the driver exhibiting the clue is drunk. The most common clues include:

- Weaving, drifting, and swerving
- Striking another vehicle or object
- Making a wide or illegal turn
- Driving without headlights on at night
- Failing to use turn signals
- Driving the wrong way on a one-way street
- Responding slowly to traffic signals
- Following too closely
- Improperly changing lanes

Speeding is one of the most common reasons for an officer to initiate a traffic stop. However, *speeding is NOT one of the 24 clues that would indicate impairment*. In approximately one out of three DWI cases I handle, my client was pulled over *solely* for speeding. In these cases, the officer is unable to say that any driving by my client was indicative of impairment. I'll ask the officer, "So out of twenty-four driving clues of impairment you are trained to look for, you saw nothing about my client's driving that would indicate he was impaired?" In such a case, the officer has to concede that during Phase One of his DUI investigation, he did not see a single clue of impairment. This is particularly helpful if the officer has followed the driver for a significant distance.

There are a few interesting catchall clues among the 24 that I generally bring up because they display *characteristics of a truly impaired driver*. One of the 24 driving clues is "appearing to be impaired." This clue includes these actions: eye fixation, tightly gripping the steering wheel, slouching in the seat, gesturing obscenely, or driving with one's head too close to the windshield or out a window. Again, it is critical for an attorney to exploit the fact that the officer is trained to look for, but did not see, any of these actions.

Another of the catchall clues is "inappropriate or unusual behavior while driving." This includes: throwing objects from the vehicle, drinking in the vehicle, urinating at the roadside, arguing without cause, or other disorderly actions. Rarely are these clues present in a DWI investigation. However, I ask an officer about each of these clues so that I can tell the judge or the jury during my closing argument, "This is what a police officer is trained to look for: a drunk. Throwing objects from the vehicle. Drinking in the vehicle. These are true clues of impairment." This method of argument emphasizes that the officer should be looking for *a drunk*, not just somebody who is nervous during a traffic stop or has poor coordination.

B. The Stopping Sequence

After the officer initiates a traffic stop, he looks for additional clues during Phase One. These clues are found during what NHTSA calls "the stopping sequence." The officer is trained to look for and make note of a driver who: attempts to flee, does not notice the officer's lights or siren, swerves abruptly or stops suddenly, or strikes a curb or object during his stop. Oftentimes my client's erratic driving can be attributed to the fact that the officer is dangerously tailgating my client, causing my client to lose focus fearing a collision is about to occur.

C. Post-Stop Indicators Of Impairment

After the stop, officers are trained to look for a number of things during the final stage of Phase One of their DUI investigation:

1. Driver has difficulty with motor vehicle controls;

2. Difficulty exiting the vehicle;

3. Fumbles with driver's license or registration;

4. Repeats questions or comments;

5. Sways or has problems balancing;

6. Leans on a vehicle or other object;

7. Slurs speech;

8. Provides incorrect information to officers;

9. Smells of alcohol; and

10. Responds lethargically to the officer's questions.

Just as it is important for the prosecutor, a.k.a. the district attorney, to punctuate when clues of DUI are present, my role is to highlight when the officer does not notice clues. If the officer only notes slurred speech and a smell of alcohol, my job is to make sure the jury knows that he is trained to look for the other clues and he did not notice those.

While almost all of the Phase One post-stop clues are common sense indicators of impairment, the smell of alcohol only shows the person has been drinking, not that the person has consumed an intoxicating amount of alcohol. An officer cannot estimate a person's impairment level or his blood or breath alcohol concentration based only on smell. Moreover, police reports frequently include a statement indicating an odor of alcohol coming from *the vehicle*. That statement is problematic, because other things in the vehicle could explain the smell, particularly if there were other passengers inside the vehicle who had been drinking. It is important that the officer is able to identify that the smell of alcohol is coming from the driver, particularly if the driver is still in the vehicle at that point.

PHASE TWO: PERSONAL CONTACT

Phase Two of an officer's training is based on personal contact between the driver and the officer. The officer is trained to develop a mental checklist of impairment indicators related to sight, sound, and smell.

A. Sight

The officer is on the lookout for a couple of things during a brief visual surveillance of the driver and vehicle:

- Bloodshot Eyes
- Alcohol Containers
- Unusual Behavior
- Soiled Clothing
- Drugs or Paraphernalia
- Fumbling Fingers
- Bruises or Bumps
- Unusual Clothing (ex. pajamas or no pants)

I constantly see "red glassy eyes" noted by an officer. Red eyes differ medically from bloodshot eyes in terms of being an indicator of alcohol impairment, and this should be addressed in cross-examination.

If the officer is not making note of these visual indicators of impairment, then the defense attorney should draw this out of the officer. In many cases, the district attorney will look at me with a sideways glance while I ask the officer if he saw the above listed items during his investigation. These are the elements that the officer is trained to examine while he determines the driver's impairment. This allows me to tell the jury: "The officer is trained to look for behaviors and clues of a truly drunk person—and they were not observed in my client."

B. Sound

In addition to the visual aspect, the officer will also listen for auditory indicators of impairment during his interaction with the driver. Does the officer hear slurred speech, an admission of drinking, or inconsistent responses? Is the driver becoming verbally abusive? Is the driver becoming angry about the circumstances? Is the driver making nonsensical statements?

People are often stopped after an accident, but they are not in the vehicle. They might be found standing on the side of the road outside of the vehicle, or discovered later at home. The officer should ask: "Have you consumed any alcohol since you were driving?" The officer is asking about the timing of alcohol consumption to determine if the individual has consumed any alcoholic since driving, does not admit to driving, or denies alcohol consumption altogether.

C. Smell

Law enforcement officers are trained to note any smells detected during their investigation, including alcohol or marijuana. Officers are also looking for "cover-up" sprays, breath mints, or any kind of smell that might disguise the use of alcohol or marijuana. It is routine for officers to ask a driver to exit the vehicle based solely on the smell of alcohol or marijuana coming from the vehicle.

D. Additional Phase Two Investigation

During Phase Two, the officers are trained to ask confusing questions or questions designed to divide the driver's attention. They will often ask for two things simultaneously, such as the driver's license and registration. If the driver only produces the license, this counts as a clue. If the driver produces an insurance card in addition to the license and registration, this counts as a clue because the driver did not respond correctly to the officer's request. By the time that an officer walks up to the window and asks for a driver's license many drivers have already pulled out their registration, license, and proof of insurance. Because the officer asked for something specific—even if the driver was simply anticipating what the officer would need—the officer may note this as a clue of impairment.

Officers are also trained to ask interrupting and distracting questions, such as: "What is your middle name? Where were you born? In which states have you been licensed in the past?" They are trying to ask confusing questions that are meant to distract the driver. They are trained not to ask questions in a chronological order. For example, an officer might ask about something that happened earlier in the day, then ask about where the driver is coming from, then ask a reverse chronological question about when the driver was born. Jumping around can distract the driver, causing more clues of impairment to be seen.

Phase Two continues with the officer instructing the driver to step out of the vehicle. During the exit sequence, the officer is looking for a driver who shows angry or unusual reactions. Angry behavior is considered another sign and will be noted as

217

an indication of impaired driving. Other clues can include the driver's inability to follow verbal directions, such as exiting from the wrong side of the vehicle or the failing to open the door. If the driver leaves the vehicle in gear upon the exit, climbs out of the vehicle (especially in low-riding cars), or uses his hand to pull himself out of the vehicle, these actions will be noted as clues. If the officer sees the driver leaning against the vehicle, sitting on the vehicle, putting an arm on the vehicle, or using the vehicle for balance, these will also be noted as signs of impairment. A driver putting his hands in his pockets a certain way or standing with his feet spread apart could also be an indicator to the officer of balancing problems. Certain standing, sitting, and kneeling positions are indicators of balancing issues.

PHASE THREE: PRE ARREST SCREENING

Phase Three is the most important stage of the officer's DWI investigation. The principal questions for the officer in Phase One and Two are, "Should I stop the vehicle?" and, "Should the driver exit?" *In Phase Three, the question the officer must answer is, "Should I arrest the driver for DUI?"*

The pinnacle of DUI detection according to NHTSA is Standardized Field Sobriety Tests (SFSTs). Officers trained in the NHTSA curriculum are taught that SFSTs have been scientifically validated to determine whether a person is above or below certain alcohol concentrations. Officers are trained to administer SFSTs in the prescribed and standardized manner, so that if any element of the test is changed, the validity of the test is compromised.

There are three SFSTs: the Horizontal Gaze Nystagmus (HGN) Test, the Walk-and-Turn Test, and the One-Leg-Stand Test. The officer can perform other tests at the roadside, but those are not standardized. One example is the Finger Dexterity Test, in which the thumb is quickly touched to the other fingers. The driver could be required to perform the Finger-to-Nose Test, in which the subject holds his arms by his sides, closes his eyes, and then brings one arm up at a time and attempts to touch the tip of his index finger to his nose. An officer might ask the driver to do an alphabet test. He could ask the driver to begin with the letter "M" and stop at the letter "S". The officer might ask the person to count backwards. An officer may also conduct the Romberg Balancing Test, which requires the driver to stand with his feet together and head slightly tilted back with eyes closed. The driver is then supposed to tell the officer when he thinks that 30 seconds have passed.

These non-standardized tests are a primary example of the "witch-hunt" nature of DUI investigations. There is extremely limited evidence that a sober person will perform these tests any better than a person with a .08 blood alcohol concentration (the *per se* impairment standard used in a majority of states). I often ask officers to give a demonstration in the courtroom of how these test are performed. I have told jurors in my closing argument to try to perform field sobriety tests during their deliberation, because *these tests are designed to fail*.

A. The Horizontal Gaze Nystagmus Test

During this test, the officer looks for a jerking or nystagmus of the eyes. Officers are trained to look for a total of six clues—three in each eye. These are:

1. Lack of smooth pursuit

2. Distinct and sustained nystagmus at maximum deviation

3. Onset of nystagmus prior to 45 degrees

The officer is trained to conduct a medical check of the eyes, hold his stimulus 12–15 inches from the driver's face slightly above eye level (too close or too far invalidates the test), move the stimulus horizontally at a very specific speed or hold the stimulus still for a definite period of time, and take detailed notes of what he sees. Of all the officers that I have cross-examined, ten to fifteen percent actually do the test correctly from start to finish. *I remind the jury that this is a test of inches and seconds and that minor deviations from the set protocol invalidate the test.*

One of the problems with the Horizontal Gaze Nystagmus test is that there are at least 30 different possible causes of nystagmus. Everyone has a natural nystagmus—a natural kind of jerking movement of the eyes—but it is not visible to the naked eye of another person in most cases. Nystagmus visible to the naked eye could be due to any number of reasons, including ingestion of alcohol.

Optokinetic nystagmus is one of the causes of visible nystagmus and is particularly important in a DUI case. It can be caused by light-related activities, such as the driver watching strobe lights, rotating lights, or seeing rapidly moving traffic in close proximity. Lights have a great deal of relevance because if the officer pulls a person over and keeps on the blue lights throughout the investigation—even if the driver is facing away—the blue lights can cause optokinetic nystagmus. Furthermore, if the officer is performing the test on the side of the road and traffic is heavy on that road, lights will quickly appear in and out of the driver's field of vision, which can cause optokinetic nystagmus to occur.

It is important for the officer to be able to differentiate alcohol induced nystagmus from other types of nystagmus. Many officers will say during their testimony, "I'm only trained in alcohol-related nystagmus. I'm not trained in these other types of things that can cause nystagmus. You'll have to ask a medical person or somebody else about that." This is a key component in our defense. If the officer cannot differentiate alcohol caused nystagmus from other causes of nystagmus, the officer may indicate a false positive in his report of the HGN Test.

There is a way to turn this test into a positive even if the officer sees all six clues and the test was administered correctly. During this test, the person is asked to stand at attention with their feet together and arms by their sides. This test takes approximately a minute to perform when the officer is following the correct timing of the test. I make it a point to ask, "So my client was able to stand with his feet together and arms by his sides for a minute? He didn't use his arms for balance, did he? He didn't sway back and forth, did he? He didn't fall over, or even step out of stance, did he? So he was able to stand straight up with no balancing problems, but you noticed a barely perceptible jerking of his eyes that could be related to 30 other causes?"

B. The Walk-And-Turn Test
The second SFST is the Walk-and-Turn Test. The officer is looking for eight clues during this test:

Clues During Instructions
1. Cannot maintain the starting position while listening to the instructions.

2. Starts performing the test before the officer finishes giving instructions.

Clues During Performance

3.   Stops walking for several seconds during the test.

4.   Does not touch heel-to-toe.

5.   Steps off the line

6.   Uses arms to balance

7.   Turns improperly at the end of the first nine steps

8.   Takes the incorrect number of steps either up or down
     the line

The officer begins this test with a set of instructions. He will tell
the driver to place his left foot on a line, whether that line is real
or imaginary, and to touch the heel of his right foot to the toe of
his left foot. The officer must tell the driver to put his arms
down by his sides and maintain this position *until the officer
gives the instruction to start the test*. There are two clues that the
officer looks for during the instruction phase. The first clue is
present if the driver starts performing the test before the officer
completes his instructions. The officer is supposed to tell the
driver as soon as he gets into starting position, "*Do not start* to
walk until told to do so." It is amazing how often an officer has
indicated that my client began the Walk-and-Turn Test too soon,
despite the officer failing to give this specific instruction. The
second clue appears if the individual has any problem
maintaining the heel-to-toe position during the officer's
instructions and demonstration.

The officer continues his instructions by telling the driver that
the test consists of taking nine heel-to-toe steps down the line,
turning by making a series of small steps, and then taking
nine heel-to-toe steps back up the line. Once the driver

begins, he is instructed not to stop walking during the test. The officer will say, "Do you have any questions? Do you understand what I told you?" Then the officer demonstrates by taking three steps and turning, while instructing the driver to take nine steps before turning.

Once the driver begins the actual test, the officer is looking for six clues (listed above). If the driver misses one single heel-to-toe step of the eighteen he takes, then the officer notes this as a clue of impairment. If the driver steps off of the line on a single step of the eighteen he takes, then the officer notes this as a clue of impairment. Stopping while walking would be another clue because the driver was instructed not to stop. Using his arms for balance or raising his arms more than six inches away from his side is another clue. Many officers note this clue, even if the arms are only slightly off of the person's body.

In many cases I have been involved with, the officer did not demonstrate how to perform the test. This is particularly important for the turn. The turn looks ridiculous and nobody turns in day-to-day life the way they are supposed to during the Walk-and-Turn. The driver is supposed to be instructed to end the nine steps on their left foot, and then pivot around on that left foot by making a series of small steps with their right foot. Without the officer giving a combination of a visual demonstration and detailed instructions, it would be almost impossible for most people to avoid exhibiting the clue of an improper turn.

During cases in which the officer does not give adequate instructions or skips the demonstration phase of the test, I remind the judge or jury: "These tests are supposed to be administered in a very *specific* way. They are *standardized* field sobriety tests and must be performed in a very specific manner.

Since the officer has not done what he was supposed to do in the instruction, this does not qualify as a *standardized* field sobriety test, and the test is invalid. The clues cannot be considered because the officer did not do what he was required to do, according to the NHTSA training that he has completed."

C. The One-Leg Stand Test

In this test, the officer instructs the person to stand with his feet together, arms by his sides, and to maintain that position while the officer gives further instructions. The officer is trained to instruct the driver to raise one foot—the driver is given the discretion on which foot to raise—six inches off the ground and keep it parallel to the ground, while keeping the other leg straight and keeping his arms by his sides. In addition to the physical portion of the test, the driver is instructed to count out loud, "one thousand and one, one thousand and two, one thousand and three," and so on, until instructed to stop by the officer. The officer should ask the driver if he understands the instructions that have been given before telling the driver to begin the test. The officer should also demonstrate how to perform the test in addition to giving verbal instructions.

The officer is trained to time this test for 30 seconds from the time that the driver raises his foot off of the ground. However, I often see in reports that officers have waited for the defendant to count to 30—i.e., "one thousand and thirty"—instead of stopping at 30 seconds. Regardless of whether my client gets to "one thousand and ten" or "one thousand and fifty" during his count, the officer is supposed to stop the test at 30 seconds. Research shows that even a non-impaired driver will have problems maintaining this position for longer than 30 seconds. It is important to limit the test to 30 seconds so that the clues pointing toward impairment will be accurate. During the test the officer looks for four clues:

1. Does the person sway while balancing?

2. Does the person use arms for balance?

3. Does the person hop with the planted foot?

4. Does the person put the raised foot down?

These are the *only* four clues that have been identified as such for the test by NHTSA. *Failing to count out loud is not a clue.* Missing a sequence in the count, such as jumping from one thousand and four to one thousand and six, is not a clue. Also, each clue only counts once even if the officer sees that clue multiple times during the test.

Limitations of the Walk-and-Turn and One-Leg Stand Tests

Age: NHTSA has identified that individuals 65 and older have difficulty performing these tests due to age. For a client aged 55 to 64, I will identify this problem to the judge or jury and say that there must be some sliding scale of physical ability. A person does not suddenly become unable to lift her leg on her 65th birthday.

Location Of Tests: These tests are to be performed on a reasonably dry, hard, level, and non-slippery surface. If the tests are performed on a hill, a steep grade, or in a gravel parking lot with uneven terrain, a false positive for certain clues could result.

Weight: A person 50 pounds overweight will likely have difficulty performing the one-leg-stand, states NHTSA research.

Injuries: A person with back, leg, or inner ear problems will have difficulty performing either test. An officer should identify and make note of any medical concerns that are present. However, officers frequently ask, "Do you have any physical limitations that would prevent you from performing field sobriety tests?" before they instruct a driver on the individual tests. Since most people have never done a field sobriety test, they normally say they are not aware of anything that would keep them from performing the test. If the officer is conducting a fair investigation, he should ask, "Do you have any medical concerns related to your legs, back, or inner ear?."

Footwear: Any person wearing footwear with two-inch (or higher) heels should be given the option to remove footwear before performing these tests. However, performing the tests barefoot could create additional reasons an individual might have trouble performing the tests to the satisfaction of the officer.

CHALLENGING THE RESULTS OF STANDARDIZED FIELD SOBRIETY TESTS

When I get the written report back from an officer that indicates why my client has failed the HGN, Walk-and-Turn, or the One-Leg Stand, there are many ways to question the officer's findings. During my cross-examination of the officer, it may become apparent that the officer did not give appropriate instructions. For example, "So you never told my client *not to begin* the Walk-and-Turn before finishing your instructions?" Perhaps the officer did not actually see the clue he indicates was present. "So you say my client used his arms for balance, but he barely raised his arms, not six inches as allowed by NHTSA?" The officer may have noted a clue that is not really a clue. "So you stated that my client exhibited the clue of not counting his

226

steps out loud during the Walk-and-Turn test, but that is not one of the eight clues identified by NHTSA during that test, is it?"

I always ask the officers if they have been trained in SFSTs by the National Highway Traffic Safety Administration. When trained by NHTSA in DUI Detection and SFSTs, officers are provided with a student manual covering the material presented during the course. The student manual provides great detail on the three stages of DUI investigation, clues that indicate impairment, and how to perform SFSTs. *That manual has become my bible for DWI defense because officers frequently do not follow their training during DUI investigations.* Whether this failure is intentional, due to laziness or forgetfulness, or a result of poor training, the consequence is the same: *bad police work.*

I use a student manual, provided to me during the NHTSA course I attended, as a measuring stick of the quality of the officer's investigation in an individual case.

During cross-examination, I always begin with questions about the particular stages of the SFSTs such as, "How did you instruct my client to perform the One-Leg Stand Test? Tell me exactly how you instruct somebody to perform that test? Are there any other instructions that you give during that test?" If the officer is giving inadequate or incomplete instructions, I can refer to my copy of the student manual and say, "You received a copy of a student manual during your training? Please look at this manual. Can you identify this manual as substantially similar to the one that you received in your training?" The officer almost always identifies that the manual is substantially similar to the one that he received during training. Then I will say, "Well, you were supposed to tell the person to keep his arms down by his sides, weren't you? But you never told him to do that, did you? You've indicated that he used his arms for balance, but you never specifically instructed him not to do so, did you? You never told the person how he was supposed to count or how high to count, did you? You never told him how he was supposed to turn at the end of his first nine steps, did you?"

During the trial, the prosecutor will often ask the officer a question such as, "You performed these three field sobriety tests?" The officer will say, "Yes, I did." The prosecutor replies, "And what did you find?" The officer will answer, "Well, I found X number of clues on the HGN, X number of clues on the Walk-and-Turn, and X number of clues on the One-Leg Stand." Almost always, the district attorney fails to obtain details about the officer's observations or the instructions given to the defendant by the officer.

Cross-examination is my opportunity to bring out the fact that my client was not properly advised of the way he was supposed to perform the tests. I'll say, "You didn't properly demonstrate to my client how to perform these tests." The student manual that the officer received during his training becomes a valuable element of our defense because we can explain to a judge or to a jury, "This clearly shows that the test is not fair, that it is not being done in a standardized, prescribed manner because the officer did not provide adequate instructions. He did not follow proper procedure in identifying the clues that he is trained to look for during these field tests."

The two main weapons of our defense include the student manual that is received by officers during their NHTSA training and the written report that the officer completes.

THE PORTABLE BREATH TEST

In most states, the officer can also administer a portable breath test (PBT). In North Carolina, officers are allowed to offer a portable breath test, provided that the device is approved by the North Carolina Department of Health and Human Services. They can use a screening device at the roadside to obtain the person's alcohol concentration. Again, I often see that officers have deviated from their training by failing to use the PBT as the last part of their DUI investigation. They are trained to use the PBT screening to confirm their decision to arrest or release the driver at the end of Phase Three. The officer can offer a portable screening test with a reading at the roadside, *to confirm that the suspect is legally impaired and the impairing substance is alcohol.*

I have had numerous cases where my client was still sitting in his car when the officer gave the PBT, even before the officer completed Phase One of investigation, let alone Phase Two or Three. This is important, because it's a deviation from the officer's training. The PBT is supposed to be offered and performed at the very end of the investigation. Otherwise, it will cause the officer's investigation to be biased.

Some of the PBT devices give an actual numerical reading of alcohol concentration, while others simply indicate a positive or negative result. In my opinion, the devices giving numerical readings will bias all aspects of the officer's investigation after the breath sample is collected. If the legal limit is 0.08 and the PBT result is 0.15, it will likely jade the rest of the officer's investigation. Instead of looking for clues of impairment *and sobriety*, the officer assumes impairment and looks only for clues of intoxication to support his conclusion. *The officer begins with the mindset that the driver is impaired and he will find the clues and indicators of impairment to justify the decision he has already made: to arrest the driver.*

In North Carolina, the numerical result of a PBT is not admissible in a DWI trial. The officer is allowed to say only whether the PBT was positive or negative for alcohol. The lack of reliability of the PBTs is the basis for not allowing the numerical results into evidence.

IDENTIFYING A GOOD DUI ATTORNEY

When searching for an attorney, I believe that the most important factor is the percentage of his practice that is devoted to impaired driving cases. A DUI is a criminal offense. Some attorneys who handle DUI cases also handle other practice areas, from family law to personal injury. Even attorneys who solely practice criminal law might handle every kind of matter, from traffic issues to felony cases. If you are facing a DUI charge and searching for an attorney, you need to know the percentage of time that each attorney you speak with devotes to DUI cases. It is important to hire an attorney who really knows the ins and outs of DUI charges.

In North Carolina, the statutes and authoritative cases related to DWI create one of the most complex areas of criminal law. Therefore, you need an attorney who really knows this practice area and this particular crime very well. The attorney's length of experience also figures into the equation. "How long has this attorney been practicing in this area of law? How many DWI cases has this attorney handled? Does he take DWI cases to trial?" If you are interested in fighting the charge against you, it is especially important to ask how many times the attorney has tried DUI cases. Some attorneys have no intention of taking DUI cases to trial. They may prefer to simply help the defendant with the plea process.

Willingness to take the case to trial is very important. Many clients come in my door and, after an extensive consultation, I tell them, "I think that, in your particular situation, pleading guilty is the best possible way to handle your case." However, if an attorney never takes any cases to trial, then this is the only advice his clients will receive—even those who have defensible DWI cases. In addition, attorneys who do not take DUI cases to trial typically aren't asking questions during the consultation that are intended to explore possible defenses to the charge.

Another important element is choosing an attorney who participates in continuing education courses directly related to DUI, whether in a teaching or learning capacity. An attorney specializing in DUI cases will be more knowledgeable because he is concerned with staying up-to-date on the latest changes to the law, as well as learning any new defense techniques.

If you are facing a DUI charge, I strongly recommend that you get an attorney to represent you. This is not a run-of-the-mill traffic charge—it has serious consequences. In North Carolina, a misdemeanor DWI can be punished by up to three years in jail. Its serious civil consequences can affect your ability to drive and therefore limit possible job opportunities. A DWI can become a permanent part of your criminal record. Some people think, "I can walk through this myself." *Don't do it!* There are too many consequences. If you cannot hire an attorney for your DUI case, you should request a public defender so that you have an attorney involved on your case. There is far too much at stake for you to represent yourself.

(This content should be used for informational purposes only. It does not create an attorney-client relationship with any reader and should not be construed as legal advice. If you need legal advice, please contact an attorney in your community who can assess the specifics of your situation.)

References:

[1]For purposes of this chapter, driving while impaired is synonymous with driving under the influence, driving while intoxicated, DWI, and DUI.

[2]Much of the content of this chapter is based on the Student Manual given to officers during NHTSA's DUI Detection and Standardized Field Sobriety Testing course.

[3]What I refer to as "clues" in this chapter NHTSA sometimes refers to as "cues." For our purposes, "clues" and "cues" of DWI are synonymous.

10

CLOSE ENOUGH FOR GOVERNMENT WORK

by Philip Wakefield, Esq.

Philip Wakefield, Esq.
Wakefield & Associates Attorneys at Law
Everett, Washington
www.philwakefield.com

Philip Wakefield attended Western Washington University, graduating in 1987 with departmental honors in political science and university honors, Cum Laude. He was awarded a scholarship to the University of Puget Sound School of Law in Tacoma, Washington and after graduating began his practice defending people charged with crimes in 1992.

After 23 years of defending suspects charged with driving under the influence he was recently asked by one of the founders of the national DUI Defense College to contribute his trial techniques on direct and cross examination of expert witnesses to be used at the national level. Mr. Wakefield is a pioneer in the development of direct examination testimony by defense expert witnesses in Washington specifically with Dr. Joseph Anderson, PhD. Mr. Wakefield's philosophy as a trial attorney is to challenge every aspect of the prosecution's case and lives by the adage that "One need not be disagreeable to disagree".

CLOSE ENOUGH FOR GOVERNMENT WORK

There are many things I can and will tell you about Driving While Intoxicated (DWI), but the most important thing you can take away from this chapter, particularly if you live in the state of Washington, is that if you are suspected of impaired driving, your state government will be testing your Breath Alcohol Content (BrAC) and putting you through an ordeal that may change your life forever, and it will do so using obsolete machinery that is fatally flawed.

In other words, the machinery used to determine whether or not your driving is impaired is probably inaccurate by as much as 10 to 20 percent. Before you folks from other states breathe a sigh of relief and conclude that your state's testing devices are accurate, understand that they, too, are probably seriously flawed. For now, I want to discuss just the Data Master 2000—Washington's device of choice (and if your state uses the Data Master 2000, pay close attention).

I know a good bit of this is painfully technical, but if and when you are charged with a DUI, these scientific facts may save you from a conviction. If nothing else, give this book to your attorney. He'll be able to use it in your defense.

The BAC Data Master 2000 was purchased and brought online by the Washington State Patrol in about 1997. At the time, the device had a warranty for defects in workmanship and parts for two years. When you do the math, you will see that the warranty on the breathalyzer machine or the breath test machine used in Washington State expired in 1999–2000. The police and law enforcement in this state have been using this machine for the last 14 years even though it is out of warranty. In fact, the machine isn't even manufactured anymore.

Since the machine is no longer made, many of the parts cannot be found. The upshot of this parts problem is that Washington State is now cannibalizing their old, non-functional machines and leaving them on a shelf somewhere, so that when their other machines break, they can use the parts on the machines that still work. I expect they have a breath-tester bone yard somewhere in Olympia. Nevertheless, they can still cobble together a machine which is 14 or 15 years out of warranty to use against you. This inspires confidence, does it not?

The second point that I want to make is that the machine, the Data Master 2000, works by something called infrared spectroscopy. The machine shoots out a beam of infrared light through a control substance and measures the value of that light at, let's say 100. Then the machine shoots out a new beam of light and it goes to this chamber that holds the suspect's exhaled breath, so that when the infrared light gets to the other side of the chamber, a second value is measured.

Let's say it is 92. In theory, the ethyl alcohol molecules, which are or are not in the breath of the person, have absorbed 8 units of that infrared light. We then conclude from the second measurement that that the alcohol content in the breath is 0.08. This level says you are drunk.

If we drew out the structure of the ethyl alcohol molecule, we'd have a CH (or hydrocarbon) molecule on the left side and the OH (or Oxygen Hydrogen) part of the molecule on the right side. The part of the molecule that registers alcohol is at the OH bond, not the CH bond, and the breath machine measures the CH bond, or the hydrocarbons. The problem with this is that there are many other molecules found within the body and in the breath the machine measures. These other molecules can confuse the machine and be mistaken for ethyl alcohol, thereby causing a false high reading.

ACETONE

Acetone is an example of one of those molecules that fool the machine. If the suspect is a diabetic or has been fasting or dieting, then his body produces acetone. Acetone is the product of the body's breakdown of fats.

Acetone can affect the Data Master reading because acetone absorbs infrared light, giving a false high alcohol reading. This is infrared light, and they use two spectrums. One of them is more sensitive to ethyl alcohol, and one is more sensitive to acetone. The Data Master is supposed to correct for this, but it cannot if it's less than 0.01 BrAC. In other words, you could have 0.0099 acetone in your system, and the Data Master won't read it. Instead, it will mistakenly attribute it to alcohol. In addition, if the acetone detector is not calibrated to differentiate alcohol levels from acetone levels, there will also be false readings. Law enforcement knows this machine will incorrectly identify the acetone molecule in your body as alcohol, so they have an acetone detector, but it may or may not be calibrated correctly. If you are dieting or have gone some time without eating for whatever reason, the acetone your body produces naturally will very likely measure as alcohol even though you've not had the first drink.

CONTAMINANTS

If the suspect has been exposed to paint thinners, paint, or other potential petroleum distillates, the accuracy of the Data Master could be affected. Other chemicals can absorb light if their molecular structure is similar. Therefore, any product that has a molecular structure similar to acetone or ethyl alcohol will be falsely interpreted by the Data Master as either alcohol or acetone.

For example, methyl ethyl ketone causes a false high reading. Methyl ethyl ketone gets into the body and into the breath by being either inhaled or absorbed to the skin. So for example, if you paint houses for a living or work in the automotive industry and you're using brake cleaners and carburetor cleaners, those will all contain methyl ethyl ketones and you may have absorbed them into your system.

A guy who's a house painter and has been painting all day may get pulled over on the way home. He could have a true BAC of a 0.000, but when he gives a breath test sample, it could show up as a 0.40. Studies written by experts B. K. Logan and S. Di Stefano have shown that the Data Master can read falsely high alcohol readings when there is no alcohol present. Even someone with asthma who regularly uses an inhaler can end up with a false high reading.

Mouth Alcohol

Anybody who has dentures, has regurgitated, or has had an incident of gastroesophageal reflux before the breath test will present with residual alcohol in the mouth. The Data Master will erroneously read it as a higher breath alcohol value. If you have dentures or gastroesophageal reflux (GERD), either could increase the amount of saliva in the mouth and increase the BrAC result due to the higher saliva alcohol concentration compared to blood alcohol. The problem with the Data Master is that it's unable to identify the presence of mouth alcohol under all circumstances. There is something called a slope detector, which may correct for the presence of mouth alcohol, but that science is suspect as well.

Essentially, if you were to chart or graph the value of the breath when the suspect first begins to breathe into the machine and it falls off quickly, that's a slope. If you had a lot of alcohol in your mouth and none in your lungs, you would initially have a high alcohol reading. Over time, as you exhale, mouth alcohol would start off high, and then your lungs would get the air out, so the reading would slope downward. Police claim the Data Master works, because they have what's called a slope detector.

Uncontrolled Biological Factors

Breath Temperature

Another problem with this machine is that it works on an old assumption that the human breath comes out of each human at the same temperature. The assumption that the human body is 34 degrees Celsius is based on a study that is probably 50 or 60 years old. Newer studies tell us the actual temperature of human body exhalation is 35 degrees Celsius, one degree Celsius higher. The problem with that is that we know through physics that for every one degree Celsius higher the human breath is, the machine registers six and a half percentage points higher than the actual BAC.

Breath temperature differs from human to human and depends heavily upon circumstances. People react to stress differently, for example. Some people are cool, calm, and collected, and other people are not. Their faces become flushed, their heart rates increase, their body and skin temperature increases. Depending upon how severely a person is affected by stress, the circumstances at the time of the arrest could influence body temperature and create a false high reading.

Breath temperature also changes during the exhalation process from 29 degrees Celsius to 36 degrees Celsius with the average being 35 degrees Celsius. A change of a two-degree increase in body temperature (measured in degrees Fahrenheit) causes an eight percent increase in alcohol measurement. Nevertheless, the Data Master assumes the subject's breath sample is at 34 degrees Celsius, if the subject were being tested accurately. It doesn't tolerate fevers associated with illness or differences in body temperature as a result of the humiliation of being arrested. If the breath sample is not 34 degrees Celsius, you may get a false high result.

Breath Volume

The Data Master also refuses to measure the volume of breath exhaled. This is also one of those little corrections that needs to be made but isn't considered important. The alcohol value of your breath can be affected by changes in breathing patterns prior to the breath test. So if somebody takes several deep breaths before giving a breath test sample, you could decrease the breath reading by up to 11 percent. Holding one's breath, on the other hand, can cause a 16 percent increase in the BrAC.

Another uncontrolled biological factor involves the human lungs. For now, let's just refer to it as the "longer you blow, the higher you go" effect.

The human body is a very complex system. In our lungs, we have little structures called alveoli. They are tiny sacs like bubbles. There are so many of them that, if it were possible to lay out all of the alveoli next to each other, they would cover an entire basketball court or a tennis court. We have lots of alveoli—600–700 million of them in an average pair of lungs.

The science that law enforcement relies upon is that the blood and the chemicals in the blood are transformed into a gas because we breathe in oxygen and breathe out carbon dioxide. The more we run, the more oxygen we need. The job of the lungs and the alveoli is to get the bad stuff out and the good stuff in, but we don't use all our lung space. Our lungs keep a large percentage of their capacity in reserve just in case we have to run away from a saber-toothed tiger. Unless you have emphysema or certain other pulmonary problems, a lot of your lung capacity is held in reserve for just such contingencies.

According to scientific studies, when a person exhales a particular volume for testing alcohol, they know that the value of the breath is different depending upon where in the breath you do your measuring. For example, the beginning of the breath has a low value, the middle has a higher value, and at the very end of the breath, the highest value of alcohol is found. The longer you blow, the higher you go.

So the question is, what is the accurate value? Is it when you start to blow, and you're a 0.04? Is it when you're in the middle of a blow, and you're a 0.075? Or is it at the end of the blow when it's a 0.12? When the Washington state toxicologists and the police are giving the test to a suspect, they are trained to encourage the suspect to blow harder and harder. "Blow! Blow! Blow!" they say. I interview people, and they are frustrated. They tell me, "Man, he had me blowing my guts out. He is standing behind me saying, "Blow, blow, blow." Do they do that because they know that the longer you blow, the higher the number?

The machine itself will typically accept a subject sample after it has received 1 1/2 liters of breath. That takes about four and a half seconds. At that point the machine says, "That's good. We have enough air." The device will be fine with a four-and-a-half second, one-and-a-half liter blow, but the law enforcement personnel are trained to encourage the suspect to blow longer and harder, which causes their BAC value to go higher. The volume is uncontrolled. So if you really wanted to do good science, you would measure the volume of the blow and the value of the breath sample from beginning to end. So you could see it begins with a 0.00, then 0.02, a 0.04, a 0.0555, and then it peaks at a 0.55. Four and a half seconds later, and now, it's a 0.12. The suspect's volume of breath was not measured. That is yet another uncontrolled biological variable.

Fixing this would be very easy, according to Doctor Joseph Anderson, who holds a PhD in biomechanical engineering from the University of Washington, Seattle. He invents breath test machines and builds them from scratch for FDA approval. (Oh, by the way, our famous Data Master 2000 is *not* FDA-approved. It's never been approved for use in humans for consumption of anything. Doctor Anderson says they could easily measure the volume of the suspect's breath, but they just don't.)

THE SIMULATOR SOLUTION

Another issue is that the devices measure human breath against a manmade solution of water and ethyl alcohol. This manmade solution is called an external simulator solution. It is mixed up in 50 gallon drums by the Washington State Toxicology Lab. Once it's all mixed up, they test it. If they come up with a 0.080, that is perfect. They bottle this solution in little quart containers, seal them and send them out to all the breath test machines throughout the state. Every 60 days, those bottles must be changed, because the solution deteriorates. Alcohol evaporates faster than the water does.

In order to emulate human breath, this liquid of ethyl alcohol and water that is kept in little quart jug next to the breathalyzer machine has a thermometer on it to manage the temperature of the solution. The solution must be kept at 34 degrees Celsius which is just about the temperature of the human body; it's hot enough that it gives off a gas. In this sealed container, there is space at the top for the gas to accumulate as the solution deteriorates. The breath test machine measures the value of the ethyl alcohol in that little hedge space for the gas. If it's reading properly, it will read 0.080. What law enforcement personnel are doing is measuring all humans against the external simulator solution's hedge space for the gas, which is, we assume, the standard unit of measure. One of the problems is that it's measuring based on grams per 210 liters, which is just an average number they pulled out of the sky. We don't know if someone's metabolism should be 210, 200, or 150. They just picked an average. And your freedom depends on the accuracy of that average.

The BAC Data Master technician—the mechanic—has stated that the breath test machine is accurate, and is always accurate to within some percentage point. The calibration with the simulator solution is supposed to be within plus or minus 10 percent. (Remember, the simulator solution is the ethyl alcohol and water mixture, cooked up at the lab in Olympia, according to the Data Master standard unit of measurement that they have pronounced to be the standard for human breath.) If the simulator solution is within 10 percent of the mean, then it is accurate enough by law. So the question is, if the simulator solution can vary between 10 percent, does that mean that the machine will be within 10 percent of accuracy when it's measuring human breath? The answer to that question is, "No." The simulator solution is, of course, different from human breath. Error will always be greater for human breath, so ten percent is the minimum amount of error. Actually, the error can be as much as 20 percent. In a world where going to jail on the testimony of one of these "accurate" machines is a reality, 20 percent is a big deal.

THERMOMETERS, SCHERMOMETERS

Another issue involves mercury thermometers and the external simulator solution. About five years ago, one Washington State employee found that an independent test confirmed that the official thermometer was way off. He went his boss and said, "We've got a problem here. I measured the mercury thermometer, and it said 34 degrees. While I was replacing it with a new digital thermometer, the new digital thermometer said that it was 36 degrees. It's off by two degrees. What should we do?"

The employee realized that this discrepancy was potentially devastating, since they had been measuring people's breath and finding them guilty and swearing that the testing was accurate. "I just figured out that about 30 percent of these mercury thermometers are inaccurate. Hey, boss, what do I do?" he asked frantically. The boss told him, "Bury it. Don't tell anybody. Switch them with the digitals and file them in a box. Don't label them."

Every time the police do maintenance on their breath machines, they are supposed to keep a record of it. In this case, they didn't. This whistle-blower's name was Anthony McElroy, of the Washington State Patrol. He considered the problem, and concluded, "You know? I'm pretty close to retirement. My boss is asking me to sell out my integrity, and I'm not going to do it. I'm going to the press."

Later, after the state had proposed a compromise solution, Anthony McElroy went to the Association of Defense Attorneys telling them that there was a problem but that the state was proposing to fix it. "Yes. We had a problem with mercury thermometers. Let's just put that aside for now, because the Washington State Patrol said that they cured the problem with the new digital thermometers." What was the ultimate answer for the "problem" convictions? It was the suppression of breath tests done in King County, Seattle, Washington for two years or more.

RELIABLE, ACCURATE MEASUREMENTS?

In the world of science and physics as related to breath alcohol testing, it is necessary to test the suspect's breath against something reliably correct. A thermometer would be good, but only if it is accurate. In a perfect world, you'd have a genetically identical, tea-totaling twin handy. Your twin would blow at the same time with you so as to have an accurate measurement of what your breath temperature and alcohol content ought to be under non-drinking circumstances. Chances are, they won't have your identical twin, so they'll measure your breath against a standard they have adopted. The unit of measurement that's used to test human breath is expressed as a GLLG/210L. That's one gram per 210 liters. That's the magical measure against which they compare human breath. State lab techs will tell you, "Well, that's generally accepted in the scientific community."

The bottom line is that human breath is compared against a standard unit of measure, and that standard unit of measure is grams per 210 liters. It's a standard that was pulled out of the air by the scientific community, who have proclaimed it to be the "average unit of measure for most humans."

Here's a thought: What if it's not 210? What if it's really 200? How does that skew your breath test result? Or, if it's not 210, what if it's 220? How does that skew the breath test result? Let's say the speed limit is 60 miles per hour. I'm driving at 60 mph. It matters whether or not I'm measuring in miles per hour or kilometers per hour. The actual speed isn't going to change, but the resulting number is going to change. In fact, 60 miles per hour equals about 96.5 kilometers per hour.

There are studies that show that this particular unit of measure could be wildly off depending on individual body structure. An 82-year-old menopausal grandmother who's diabetic is going to have a different body structure and chemistry than you'll find in a 19-year-old male aerobics instructor, but they use the "one size fits all" unit of measure of grams per 210 liters.

Electronic Drift

There are a couple of people who maintain these machines in Washington State who are called BAC Data Master Technicians. If they ever replace the Data Master, these master technicians will probably change their title to something even fancier like maybe BAC Czars. I call them mechanics. When you interview this person who tries to work on these machines, it goes something like this:

"Where'd you get your PhD?"
"I didn't."
"Well, Master's?"
"No."
"Bachelor's?"
"No."
"Really? You didn't go to college?"
"No."
"Well, where'd you learn about this machine?"
"The police taught me. They sent me to a course."
"Okay. So you're here as an expert to testify that this machine is accurate, and it's accurate because the police taught you that it's accurate, right?"
"Right."
"Did you ever write an article about maintaining the machine's accuracy and have it reviewed by your peers and published in a scientific journal? Or is there

anything that you've read that confirms that it's accurate?"

"Nope."

"All right. How often do you tune this thing up?"

"Once a year."

"Really? Once a year? Are you familiar with the concept of electronic drift?"

"Nope."

If you know what the proper calibration should be, you could measure where your machine is and adjust it back to where it ought to be. With the correct information, you can calibrate a machine accurately, whether it's a small block Chevy V8 or a Data Master. However, with use and in time, electronic machinery will drift away from its correct calibration. It's called electronic drift.

If you're a scientist, and you wanted to be sure the machine was working properly, you would bring in the machine and measure it electronically. You determine its performance, and you would record your findings. That way, you could know how far off it was. Then you would readjust it to the manufacturer's specifications, and as a mechanic, you could say, "It's accurate." Then you would send it back out into the field until its next maintenance interval, which is a year.

Not so much, here in Washington State. Here is the procedure that the Washington State Patrol uses when they bring the machine back: they bring it in, they turn it on, they warm it up, and they adjust it to the manufacturer's specifications. In other words, there's never going to be a record that it was off.

Do you see the problem with that?

It's obvious that with the Data Master, we'll never know if there was electronic drift or not because the quality assurance program does not require them to perform testing—or record test results from the machine when it's first brought in from the field —to determine whether or not there has been electronic drift.

Then there's the sworn accuracy of the external stimulator solution we talked about earlier. When the lab technicians mix up these big vats of external simulator solution for distribution, they have to certify them. They have to say, under oath, "I mixed this stuff, I tested it, and I swear under oath that it's accurate." They send that authenticating document to their boss who says, again, under oath, "I was there, and I was watching. I watched them test it, and it's accurate. I swear under penalty of perjury."

Eventually, there was a Washington State Toxicology employee who blew the whistle on the head of the toxicology lab as well. The problem with the lab lady's particular testimony was that Ms. Toxicology Lab Honcho wasn't even in the state at the time in question. Not only did the state get caught by a whistle-blower because their mercury thermometers were inaccurate, but there was another disgruntled employee, who said, upon her departure, in essence, "Hey, by the way, when our boss was swearing under penalty of perjury that she was here and watching us mix this solution and she certified under penalty of perjury that it was accurate, she wasn't even in the state." Seattle Times got this information through the Public Records Act and was able to prove that the woman was actually testifying in Washington, DC on another matter at the time that she claimed to be watching in the Washington lab facility while they tested the stuff. Oops.

In a nutshell, when it comes to this particular non-FDA-approved breath testing machine, there are a few problems. In the interest of absolute accuracy, we could measure temperature, but we don't. We could also measure the volume of the sample, but we don't. We could even measure the correct side of a molecule with the infrared spectroscopy, but we don't. My expert, Dr. Joseph Anderson, who has expertise in respiratory physiology and breath testing, has an opinion about the accuracy of the breath test and its reliability. Doctor Anderson's opinion is that even if the Data Master is operating correctly, the breath test reading is neither an accurate nor reliable indication of the breath alcohol, because the variations caused by the human body are neither measured nor corrected for. The standard of scientific accuracy is not met.

The machine is not accurate, because of the uncontrolled biological factors. It is not reliable because it's out of warranty, and no parts are available for it anymore. The machine isn't made anymore. None of this is based on good science. If the machines were reliable, somebody else would use them. Hospitals would use them. Somebody other than the police department would use them.

When I'm picking a jury I to like to use the following analogy:

> *"What if the IRS invented a tax lying machine, and instead of a breathalyzer, it's called a tax-a-liar? It's going to see if you're lying on your taxes. They invent this machine, and they train a mechanic to make sure this machine works, but the mechanic's never been to college. Nevertheless, we may rest easy in the assurance that the IRS taught him all about this machine.*

"This new IRS machine works like this: you fill out your tax form and feed it into the machine. The machine reads your tax form and decides whether it's accurate or not. The machine says your tax return is acceptable if it is within 10 percent of the national mean."

In terms of breath analysis, the breath limit is a 0.080. Let's say the first time you blow a 0.088, which is within 10 percent. You say, "Well, wait a minute. I know I'm not over the limit."

The man says, "Alright. Give us another breath sample. We'll try it again."

This time, it comes out as a 0.072. That's under the limit. You say, "Thank God." This 0.072, that's within 10 percent of 0.080, right? That's close enough for government work.

In other words, when using the BAC Data Master 2000, you have to provide two samples, and the samples, to be considered valid, have to be within 10 percent of their mean average. So, the first time, when you blow a 0.088, you're a criminal. The next time, when you blow a 0.072, you're not a criminal.

The Washington Administrative code says that as long as the breath test samples are within 10 percent of the mean average, they're valid samples. That's close enough for the government.

That should scare the crap out of everybody in America.

Somehow, though, folks don't seem to get it.

(This content should be used for informational purposes only. It does not create an attorney-client relationship with any reader and should not be construed as legal advice. If you need legal advice, please contact an attorney in your community who can assess the specifics of your situation.)

Made in the USA
San Bernardino, CA
26 February 2015